The Boy Who Outwitted Mengele

Michael (Miki) Popik
and William L. Simon

Cover art & design by David Folkman

Edited by Monet Euan

ISBN 978-1-973-57516-0 (pbk)

Printed in the United States of America

For Esther,
and for Frida, Anita, and Vivian

CONTENTS

PART ONE

FROM PEACE TO WAR

Growing up in the early 1930s, I knew nothing of the harsh treatment Jews had suffered throughout the centuries. Was I better off not knowing? The truth might have prepared me more for the horrors I was to face.

In the small town of Levice in the Slovak part of Czechoslovakia, some families went to church, and some went to synagogue. It made no difference to us. My boyhood friends were Christians as well as Jews. Together we swam in the town's river, played what Americans call soccer, and went to see movies like *The Wizard of Oz* and the Shirley Temple films. In winter, we walked up the nearby hills together, strapped skis to our shoes, and careened down the hills with glee. When the river froze, we all went ice skating.

My father, William, owned a small trucking business with two non-Jewish partners. It provided enough income that we didn't know hunger and had all the food and clothing we needed. He dressed very well and loved sports, especially soccer, which he played on a local team. One of the things I think he was most proud of was that he served in the Reserves of the Czech army with the rank of Sergeant. I can still call up a picture in my mind of how handsome and impressive he looked in his uniform, ready to leave for a weekend of duty.

My mother, Frida, was a beautiful, happy woman. In my memory of those days, she always had a reassuring, self-confident smile on her face. Besides Czechoslovakian, she and my father also spoke Hungarian and some German.

My parents had produced three sons. I was the middle child. My brother, Andrew, was two years older than me, and I had a baby brother, Gabi.

We were not particularly religious, but Saturday mornings we went to temple together. We usually spent Sundays with friends, often picnicking on the riverbank and swimming while the adults played cards. In the summers, we took trips to other parts of Czechoslovakia and Hungary to visit relatives and friends.

I can't really call her a girlfriend, but there was one good-looking girl I had special feelings for and she for me. We liked to sit next to each other, talking and sharing secrets. She was a shiksa, a non-Jewish girl or woman. But it made no difference to us that we were different religions, and it made no difference to our parents. I think that says a lot about the lack of religious prejudice in those days—those comfortable, happy pre-war days.

Since neither of my parents was very religious, I never learned much Hebrew. As I approached age thirteen, the preparation for my bar mitzvah was a challenging time. I spent a few months in intensive study with the rabbi. We met three days a week after school to learn the Torah passage I read in Hebrew on the Saturday of my thirteenth birthday.

So we were more-or-less an average family, living a simple, enjoyable life in a democratic country where we were free of want and free of fear. I recoil when I think of those innocent times before the war. The life I knew that seemed so happy and untroubled was too soon to collapse.

Hitler came to power in 1933 when I was only three years old. He had begun building his Nazi war machine. In 1938, his troops invaded a portion of Czechoslovakia known as the Sudetenland. During the early years of the war, we were untouched, and the truth was hidden from us. Our news reports came entirely from the Nazi controlled media. Our local newspapers carried no stories of "Kristallnacht," known in English as, "The Night of Broken Glass," when synagogues were torched, along with Jewish homes and businesses. Nor were there stories of Hitler's troops and supporters rounding up some thirty-thousand Jewish men—the first of the concentration camp victims.

The changes in our lives began gradually. I remember overhearing conversations between my parents and their friends. They talked politics and spoke about things like Jews being sent to labor camps. The tone of their voices scared me. But I would go to sleep, and by the time I woke up in the morning, I forgot what I heard the night before.

One afternoon, I played marbles with a group of my friends from school in our backyard. We were laughing, shouting at each other, and being very noisy. I was so proud of myself because I won marbles from the other boys and had an impressive collection in front of me.

My father came out to the yard. He took it all in and looked distressed. He leaned over to me and said very quietly, "Give them back their marbles."

"No," I said defiantly. It was the way we always played; if you win a marble, you keep it. "They're mine," I insisted. "Why should I give them back?"

He leaned even closer and said, "Because their parents will say you stole the marbles." I came to understand only much later.

Soon after, the boys at my school decided to put together a marching band. They needed a drummer, and one of my friends said he would teach me how. Then, one of the other boys said, "You're no good. You can't be in the band." He said it in a way that let me know what he really meant, "You can't be in our band because you're Jewish."

In that moment, I understood. I understood the truth that permeated the atmosphere and surrounded me, but I had refused to acknowledge: I wasn't one of the gang anymore. The world had been divided into them and us. I was one of the others, the excluded. I was a Jew-boy. The world had changed. We had become the hated. Hitler had no place in our lives, but we had become his victims.

In September 1938, France and Great Britain, hoping to avoid war, foolishly signed a pact with Hitler known as the Munich Agreement. It allowed Germany to take control of portions of Czechoslovakia. About six months later, on one unhappy day, units of the Hungarian army arrived in our town. The war had come to Levice.

At first, life went on as usual. Most of the families at our temple didn't like this, but some actually approved of the soldiers and saw nothing wrong with the decisions being made for the town by Hungarian army officers.

On September 1, 1939, Germany invaded Poland. The Second World War had started in earnest. My father was away on duty with the Czech army unit. We didn't know where. We didn't know if he was safe, and we didn't know what he was doing. One thing we did know was that he was wrong—everything was not going to be okay.

Portrait of my mother, Frida, 1923

Weeks went by with no word from him. As hard as mother tried to face each day by carrying on with our normal routine, I heard her sobbing at night. I think sometimes knowing nothing is worse than receiving bad news.

Finally, a letter arrived from my father, but it said nothing about where he was or what he was doing. He said he was safe. This was not reassuring.

About several months after my father departed with the other local soldiers, they finally returned. My father said that when they were dismissed, they were told they had to walk home. Walk! It was a distance of many, many kilometers. Worn out and without food, except for what they could beg from townspeople, they struggled and dragged themselves along for an entire month.

My father, the man I had always been so proud of and admired, my model of what it meant to be a grown-up, now seemed beaten. We longed to do something to reassure him, to restore the pride he once felt. But what could we do? Nothing. We felt helpless.

By 1941, many of our Christian neighbors became openly insulting toward us. Kids, who had been my friends, dressed like the youngsters in Hungary we saw in the newspapers, proudly strutting down the street in their uniform-like black outfits and hurling insults at us.

In 1942, new rules were established. All the Jewish families had to sew Jewish stars on a sleeve of each sweater and jacket. We were no longer allowed to travel. We were no longer welcome in the homes of our Christian friends.

Soon another regulation was announced. Jews could no longer own a business. Some of the Jewish men found jobs in grocery stores, butcher shops, and lawyers' offices. My father was demoted to a worker in his own company instead of a partner and owner. Now he was paid like the other employees. We had to adjust to living on much less income, which meant cutbacks in the quantity and quality of our food and clothing.

The only clothing available cost more than before, and it was shabby and poorly made of inferior material. New shoes fell apart almost before you got them out of the store. My parents became uncommonly difficult, impatient, and nervous. The whole household was upset. We could no longer afford the many things that had been routine before.

One day, some boys arrived in our hometown. They had escaped a savage massacre near Krakow. They told us that one morning, eight hundred Jews from their town, including their own parents, were driven into the synagogue, which was then set on fire. They heard the screams and cries as most of the town's Jews were burned alive.

Our leaders told us this couldn't be true, and we should not believe such stories. But we cried as it was clear those boys were truly suffering, and they walked all the way here from Krakow, some three hundred kilometers (about two hundred miles).

The following year, we learned from the BBC that Hitler was losing the war on all the fronts. Naturally, we were very happy. We didn't know that we were—by some odd chance—the only Hungarian Jewish community still living in our own homes. The conditions were miserable, but we were free and unaware of what was happening all around us. We had remained mostly untouched by the true horrors so many others faced. Even so, my older brother and I heard our parents share their despair over the situation. In time, we learned that many Jews in neighboring countries had been rounded up and sent to concentration camps.

Stories reached us of Jewish families who fled to Palestine. My parents decided we would try to do the same, but their decision came too late. The next ship to Palestine was fully booked, and we discovered there would not be any others.

Then, in March of 1944, as spring approached, an order came from the Hungarian government. A section of about three blocks by three blocks was fenced off and designated as a ghetto, and all the Jewish families had to move there.

The situation quickly became dark and desperate. The Popik family was crowded into a home which we shared with four other families. Fifteen of us were packed into a space meant for a single family. We were provided with very little food. My mother couldn't hide her fear and sense of desperation. Some twenty-two hundred of us were crammed into this small ghetto.

The Hungarian government, which had become an ally of Hitler early on, tried to break away. Hitler responded by sending the German army into Hungary. The Hungarian president was placed under house arrest, and Germany took over.

With the Nazis in charge, at Passover in 1944, we received orders to move again, this time to a sprawling former army complex. This place was much worse than the ghetto. It was like being in a bad jail. The air was rank, there was no place to exercise, and most of the day was taken up with receiving our rations and preparing meals. We had to cook each meal by building a fire as a makeshift stove with only a few pieces of wood. The crowded ghetto apartment we lived in just before seemed almost luxurious now.

The soldiers that guarded us were cruel and hardly human. Anyone who looked as if he had been prosperous was tied up with his arms straight out and interrogated: Where did you leave your money? Where did you hide your gold? If the answers turned out to be untrue, he was tied up again and questioned until he collapsed.

Simply staying alive had become a struggle. The sole touch of humanity and kindness was the generosity of some families living nearby. The Slovak people were much more accepting of Jews than any of the other countries in the area. At night, brave neighbors slipped into our camp to bring food. This wasn't out of the kindness of their hearts. Our parents still had money and were able to pay these night visitors. Still, they came at great risk. They would have suffered severely if caught.

THE HELL CALLED AUSCHWITZ

We lived in this soul-destroying army complex for only a few weeks when we received new orders. We were to pack up once again and prepare to move to a "labor camp" somewhere in Hungary.

The next day, we took our belongings and were marched to the train station. There, we found most of the Christian population standing on the sidewalks, ready to watch the Jews ejected from their city. Some of the neighbors cried, while others laughed. They were obviously pleased that we were being taken away.

I still remember the faces of some of the boys and girls who had been my friends as they stood there smiling, laughing, and calling out at us. They clearly enjoyed the scene. How they had changed in such a short time. It was painful and humiliating, but it was the new reality.

When we came to the train station, there was no passenger train. There were only the cattle boxcars that have come to symbolize the coldheartedness of those years. Bewildered, I asked my father, "They are going to transport us with boxcars?"

Father was a very practical man. He responded, "It's wartime. Maybe they don't have enough regular trains." He tried to reassure us and his friends, "They say we are going to Hungary. It is a small country. We will get to our destination in a day, at most a day and a half."

My father and the other respected men told us that to stay alive and to stay together as families, we had to obey the orders of the soldiers wearing Hungarian and German uniforms. "Those animals are not soldiers," my father said to the others. "To be a soldier is an honor, and these men have none. They are either born or trained murderers."

We were ordered onto the train with sixty-five people per boxcar. Many of the women and girls began sobbing. There wasn't even enough room to sit, but somehow we made space for the elderly to sit. The rest of us stood, tightly squeezed in with our bodies pressed against one another—and then the train just sat there. It wasn't until after nightfall that the Hungarians came and closed the heavy doors.

The train started to move, and we all cried. We had been forced to leave our homes, lost the friends we had loved for so many years, and were packed together like the cattle these cars were meant to carry—cars that reeked of the smell of animals and their waste. The condition in the train was so bad that the religious elders among us prayed and continued to pray to God through every waking hour. Others agonized over why God would allow this to happen if he really cared for the Jews, and some prayed for the Allied bombers to come and destroy us.

There was one bucket in the corner of the train car. For the men and us boys, we could easily take care of our personal needs in the bucket. But for the women and the girls, to do their business in a bucket in the presence of sixty-five other people was shameful. Of course no one looked at the person on the bucket, yet for the females it must have been humiliating. Even worse, we were from such a small town that every Jewish person knew every other Jewish person.

Hours went by with no one able to sleep amidst the babies crying, the elderly moaning in discomfort and pain, and the unceasing noise of the squeaky wheels. We were living an unimaginable nightmare.

It began to get light, the dawn of a new day of fear and uncertainty. Around noon the train finally stopped, and the heavy doors were rolled open by Hungarian soldiers. On the platform we saw for the first time squads of the German SS, the vicious "Schutzstaffel." We all knew from the radio of their cruel, heartless, and murderous treatment of all minorities. Seeing them in the flesh for the first time was very frightening.

But what were they doing at this train station? If we were just being moved to a new camp, why was the SS bothering with us?

Commands were shouted to send young men with a blanket for some food. The boys came back with food, and once again those heavy doors were rolled closed and locked. The train started up.

My father's prediction of a day and a half of travel came and went. The second day rolled into a third, then to a fourth. Hours of tedium, of crying women and screaming babies, of intolerable hunger and unbearably foul odors seemed like they would never end. It doesn't take long for sixty-five people to fill one small bucket with human waste that could only be emptied at the midday stop for food and water. The smell from the bucket was sickening yet inescapable.

We slept for twenty to twenty-five minutes at a time and woke up to find this was not a nightmare but a reality. By the fourth day, even my father was bewildered as to where we might be. Where could they be taking us?

On the fifth morning, at daybreak, I woke up early. I saw my father standing at one of the small openings in the corner of the car. When he turned around and I saw how miserable he looked, I wanted to cry. I had never seen him look like that. The once strong and proud army sergeant had changed completely. Even after so many years, I can still see the face that frightened me so that morning. I wanted to ask him why he looked so miserable and scared, but I was afraid to ask him anything that would make his pain worse. My mother woke up and couldn't resist. She saw his face and asked, "What's happening?"

He answered loud enough for others to hear, "We are in Poland." Poland was a black hole—the Polish Jews were murdered by the thousands every day. We had all heard the horror stories about the people being treated brutally and worked to death.

All hell broke loose in the boxcar. Some people wanted to commit suicide, and we had to hold them back. A young pregnant woman managed to cut her wrists. We took shirts and quickly bandaged her wrists, so she did not bleed to death. We saved her life, not knowing she would soon be sent to the crematorium with her unborn child to die a painful death.

I flashed back to the boys from Poland who arrived in our town with their story of the eight hundred Jews who were rounded up and burned alive in their synagogue. I remembered their description of the screams and shouts they heard as their parents burned in the fire. And I remembered that our Jewish leaders told us not to believe these stories or befriend youngsters who told such horrid tales. I wondered, what would these revered men say now?

Father gathered a few of the men who had army experience. They sat in a corner and worked out a plan. The next time the train stopped, the men and every strong woman, armed with kitchen knives, would leap off the train and attack the guards, hopefully killing a few and taking their guns. Meanwhile, the rest of us were to run off and escape into the Carpathian Mountains. We would all run, every single man, woman, and child with babes in arms. If we died, if every one of us died, we all knew it would be better than the Hell we surely faced.

At mid-afternoon, the train slowed at last. My father looked out the window and confirmed we were still in Poland. I remember the look of terror on his face. Panic broke out once again. We knew about the Germans "exterminating" people from the ghettos. I think every person old enough to understand shared the same feeling—*this is the end.*

I pushed my way toward the window slits with some of the other boys. We saw a huge sign in Polish:

Oświęcim

We did not know that this was the Polish name for a site that would go down in history as one of the cruelest places in the history of mankind: Auschwitz.

When the train stopped, I read the fear in my parents' faces as they clung to each other and to us, their children. The doors were thrown open revealing a scene that made the blood run cold.

Soldiers with dogs and guns shouted, "SHNELL RAUS, SHNELL RAUS..." This was German for, "Fast, out." We grabbed our belongings, and they shouted at us, "Leave it! You don't need those things anymore."

From the train platform, we saw hundreds and hundreds of gray barracks with tiny windows below the roofs. In the distance, chimneys, like at a factory, spewed out heavy smoke that rolled over the camp with ashes falling everywhere. The odor of the smoke from the chimneys was sickening. Many from our train—the women, the young, and the aged—would soon find out the true nature of that foul smoke.

All these years later, to recall that sight and odor is still terrifying. The confusion of the next few seconds is so hard to explain. Off the train, lines were already formed. One was for mothers and their children, the elderly, and anyone who seemed sick. A much shorter line was for able-bodied men and women. Mothers pushed to the left, and grandparents pushed to the right.

Though thirteen and small for my age, when I saw my mother and my two-year-old brother sent to the long line, I started at a run, afraid for them and desperate to protect them somehow. Within two steps, my father locked my wrist with an iron grip. "No," he said sternly. "You are coming with the men. You are a bar mitzvah boy."

Only much later would I recognize this as a crucial moment. With that command, he unknowingly saved my life.

The three of us waved to my mother and my little brother, and they waved back until they disappeared behind one of the huge factory buildings emitting the smoke. "They are going to the children's camp," one of the guards told us. We were reassured.

Thanks to God we did not know they were going directly to the crematoriums. If we had known, the Nazis would have had to slaughter all of us right there.

Those brief waves were the last we would ever see of each other. This moment haunts my memory today, as it will for the rest of my conscious life.

Someone must have whispered something to my father about my short height, or maybe he watched who was being sent to which group and made the discovery on his own. Risking his life, he suddenly pushed through the dense crowd and ran back to the cattle car we had been in. Moments later, he was back with a pair of my mother's winter boots. He held them low, so none of the guards saw them. He handed them to me and said, "Put these on."

I told him, "They are *lady's* boots."

He said softly but in a voice that was a stern command, "PUT THEM ON!"

I sat on the ground, pulled off my shoes, and while I put on the boots, he grabbed my shoes and threw them over the crowd far away. As soon as the boots were on my feet, he pulled me upright and yanked my trousers down till the bottoms were close to the ground, hiding most of my feet. The boots added about two inches to my height. It was enough to make me look old enough to be sent with the men and older boys.

The line we were standing in began to move, and we slowly made our way toward the SS officers at the front. The officer in charge signaled who was to join the group of prisoners on our right and who was to join the group on our left.

When we reached him, I stretched myself tall and was made taller by the boots. The Nazi looked at my father and snapped, "How old is he?"

My father answered in German, fifteen, adding two years to my real age. The officer signaled my father, Andrew, and me to go to the shorter line. This was the safe line where prisoners eventually became factory workers.

All of my friends my age and all of my schoolmates were sent to the other line. My father's instinct for survival saved my life again in a matter of moments.

I learned later that the tall, self-possessed German officer who let me go with my father and brother was a man who would become infamous—the savage Nazi butcher, Dr. Josef Mengele. Thanks to my father, I cheated Mengele. I outwitted him.

When the sorting was over, Capos led us through this huge camp, a walk that felt like it would never end. All along the way, hundreds and hundreds of prisoners rushed out from their barracks, crowding the barbed wire fence that separated them from us. The site was horrifying. The men looked to be one hundred and fifty years old and were so emaciated that they were barely more than skeletons. It was like watching dead men walking, and it was painful to look at them.

They were our Jewish brothers, and they were starving, calling out, and begging us to throw some food over the fence to them. We would have given them everything, but we had been ordered to leave all belongings in the boxcars including the food we left behind. If only we had known that starving people were waiting for a small piece of bread, we would have stuffed our pockets. But we didn't know and had nothing to share.

My father made no comment, but I'm sure he must have been thinking, "Is that what we are going to look like in a month or two?"

We felt relief when we passed them because it was the scariest, most unpleasant thing we had ever witnessed.

We arrived at a brick building and were told to take showers. This was welcome because we were so filthy from traveling. Once we undressed, a team of young prisoners with all kinds of cutting tools shaved off all the hair from the top of our heads, sideburns, and beards. I looked around and could barely tell one man from another, people I had known all my life. I felt adrift, stranded as if among strangers, which made it all the more frightening.

From there, we were sent into the showers, but this wasn't anything like a shower at home. We were made to walk through quickly without soap or scrubbing; we just got a brief wet down. We came out the other side dripping wet and found there was nothing to dry off with. There were no cloth towels or paper towels, not even a little toilet paper.

As each one of us emerged, another group of prisoners doused us all over with some smelly powder (probably some kind of DDT). They gave us prison clothing, a top and bottom similar to pajamas but so rough and stiff they were hard to put on. And the shoes were worse than the clothing. With soles of solid wood about an inch thick and toppings made of an uncomfortable canvas, it felt impossible to walk.

I was bewildered and frightened standing there among all those naked men trying to get into their stiff, rough clothing. By then it was already late at night. I think every man and boy among us must have been as confused and scared as I was.

After another hour or more, one of the prisoners in charge of us approached and offered me a sandwich. *Why is he offering a sandwich just to me? Why isn't everybody else getting a sandwich?*

Looking back, I think it must have been a small touch of human kindness for the young child I was, so much younger than any of the others.

I told him, "Thank you, I don't want it."

But my father came close and whispered, "Miki, take the sandwich. Here you are in a prison."

When my father told me I was in prison, I felt so confused. I couldn't believe it. But I still couldn't bring myself to take a sandwich offered to me by the vicious people in charge of us.

These vicious men were known as Capos. Capos were prisoners given authority, good food, and warm clothing, and required to make the life of prisoners as miserable as possible. Some were German criminals, others the dregs of mankind—people willing to torture, brutalize, and drive prisoners to their death in exchange for a variety of privileges. Yet there were a few among them who retained some shred of humanity.

I eventually learned that the camp we were in, called Birkenau, was part of the complex that made up the vast Auschwitz concentration camp.

We were taken to the barracks called the Gypsy camp. There were about eighteen to twenty-thousand German Gypsy families living together in this one camp. Soon after our arrival, all of the Gypsies were taken to the crematorium one night. That was how Hitler ended the history of Gypsies in Germany. I learned later that he hated the Gypsies almost as much as he hated Jews.

When we reached the Gypsy barracks, my day ended with yet another shock. The adults were directed to one building, the teenagers to another. I was separated from Andrew and from my father, who was my idol and my strength. Without him, I did not know who to trust, how to act, or what to do.

It had long since become dark, and we had been given nothing to eat or drink. We were to sleep on a bare concrete floor on a very cold night. They lined us up in three rows with only a little space between each boy. We were then ordered to sit on the floor, with legs apart, straddling the boy in front. And then, on command, everyone was to fall back, roll over onto our sides, with our heads on a foot of the boy behind us. The lights went out. I thought the sound of boys crying would make sleep impossible, but thankfully I fell asleep almost instantly.

Around sunrise the next morning, a flock of Capos came in shouting and kicked us awake. They told us breakfast would be at eight. What they delivered was not breakfast but quarts of filthy warm water that smelled and tasted so foul, it was painful to swallow, almost sickening. I heard gagging sounds from every direction. The Capos laughed and claimed they were doing us a favor because filthy water is all that we would get, and they were helping us get used to it. The most painful part of this was that most of the Capos were Jewish. Criminals and crooks, yes, but Jewish criminals and crooks. Being mistreated at the hands of fellow Jews was worse than being mistreated by the SS.

The rest of the morning was a nightmare. Every thirty to forty minutes, we had to "FALL IN FOR ROLL CALL." In our thin, itchy, pajama-like striped uniforms, we lined up. The Capos called us the filthiest names conceivable. It was so offensive that we almost couldn't stand it. They shouted at us that we were not human, and we were hated animals. They beat this man and that one for crimes no worse than a groan or a sob, and then, shouted warnings that we better get used to being hated and getting beaten.

But the worst part of the first day was the hunger. We had not eaten a real meal for two days. Constant hunger drives you toward insanity and can indeed turn you into an animal.

Finally, after so many roll calls and so many beatings, "lunch" arrived. "Lunch" was warmed-over garbage. Garbage! It smelled like garbage, looked like garbage, and tasted like garbage. Other boys who had been in the camp longer were emaciated and clearly starving. They dove into eating the garbage as if they were enjoying it. Enjoying garbage! My friends and I, having just arrived, saw them swallow it as if they were happy. We were unable to eat and gave our food to others.

The afternoon was filled with more roll calls but not quite as many beatings. The evening meal at last brought some food we could eat. Bread, one loaf for eighteen boys. It was a very unusual bread, odd tasting but manageable. It seemed to be made from various kinds of grains crushed together into a mass that was soggy even after baking.

It didn't take long to figure out that a major ingredient of this bread was sawdust, maybe fifteen or twenty percent. We had to eat carefully because the sawdust wasn't always ground up well. We often found small chips of wood in the bread.

As the days passed, people all around me started getting diarrhea. In the concentration camp, diarrhea was a death sentence because you become weak very quickly. When ordered to fall in for a prisoner count, you cannot stand on your legs for very long. So they send you to the infirmary.

People who went to the infirmary never came back. I saw one friend after another sent to the infirmary, and it was the last I ever saw of them.

Every night, packed body to body for warmth, sobs came from every direction, now and then interrupted by the screams from a nightmare. But even those chilling sounds were reassuring, announcing to each of us, "You are not alone in your suffering and despair. And you are still alive."

Most of my fellow prisoners, like myself, no longer believed in the goodness of man that our religion taught us. Even in my childhood, with so little understanding, I no longer believed there could be a God. How would God permit all I saw going on in this miserable place?

Did I want to stay alive in this Hell? Yes. For me, the instinct to survive was too strong, and my father set the example for surviving.

In those early weeks, there was no work for us. The days were filled with idleness, interrupted every hour or so by shouts to fall into ranks and call out in turn our assigned numbers. However, sometimes we were made to stand for what seemed like hours, while the Capos found reasons to savagely beat anyone who no longer had the strength to stand erect or who had become sick or feeble.

Though my father and brother were assigned to different barracks, theirs was adjacent to mine, so we were able to spend time together every day. My father offered words of support, hope, and advice that I now know he could not have believed but offered as the only medicine in his power to provide. They were lies given as lifesavers. He did not want me to become one of those we had all seen—prisoners who ran to the electric barbed wire fence and threw themselves onto it, choosing death as a salvation from cruelty and torture.

SAVED FROM THE GAS CHAMBER

After six weeks of this horrible life, my father and my brother came to see me one morning. My father told me, "Miki, we are going to be transferred to a labor camp in Germany, a place called Dachau." I found out later that Dachau wasn't just a labor camp, it was a murder camp.

There were only a few minutes before they had to leave. My father sat down with me and Andrew in a corner and gave me very important advice that saved my life over and over again. In fact, he didn't give me advice. He gave me orders, orders from a sergeant to his young son.

He told me many personal things. Of course, he told me how much he loved me and how proud he was of me, but he mostly focused on crucial guidelines to survive in this place. He told me something along these lines, "Every day in the morning when you get your water ration, you're going to wash your face. Half of the water you're going to drink, but the other half you're going to use for rubbing your cheeks and scrubbing them so you look like a healthy, young boy! Like a soldier. And with a little bit of the water, always try to clean your uniform."

And then he told me, "God forbid if you get diarrhea. Don't mention it to anyone. Not to anyone! Just go to one of the boys who pick up the food from the kitchen. Choose a boy you think you can trust. Tell him that at night when you get your bread, you will share a piece with him. Tell him you will do this if he will steal for you from the kitchen a small chunk of burnt-wood charcoal. When you get the charcoal, chew it. This will relieve your stomach problems."

He told me one other thing I had already figured out, "If the Capos learn you have diarrhea, they will send you to the infirmary." He did not have to explain. He knew I understood.

The last thing he told me was, "If you see that you have a chance to volunteer for anything, raise your hand! Promise me you will volunteer for anything no matter what."

I promised.

Andrew and I sat next to each other crying as we listened to my father. He reassured my father, "Don't worry. Miki is going to take care of himself."

Before they left, they kissed me, and I kissed them in return. My father's last words to me were, "Remember, Hitler is losing the war. We'll see you at home soon."

Then it was time for them to go. My father and my older brother. I watched them walk away. It was the last time I ever saw them.

It is only because of my father's instructions, and a little bit of luck, that I am here today. Father saved my life tenfold.

After they left, Mengele came to select some of the children in my group. We knew by then how dangerous this was. We heard terrifying stories about Mengele selecting children for all kinds of horrible experiments, and we never saw any of them again. Friends in the camp warned each other, "Never volunteer. All kinds of terrible things could happen to you if you volunteer."

Mengele asked, "Who has some experience in metal work?" All my closest friends stood perfectly still. It didn't matter to me what my friends thought was the only wise choice in this moment. I had those orders from my father to volunteer. I promised him.

I raised my hand. Mengele walked down the rows toward the few boys who had their hands up, boys older than me and taller than me. As he approached, I looked directly into his eyes like a good soldier, but he walked by. I followed him with my eyes. After three or four steps in front of me, he stopped.

Very unusual, Mengele doesn't stop. In the camp, he is God.

He took a few steps back toward me.

He slapped me on my cheek and said in German, "Jump."

It meant, "Go to the truck." I did, and he selected some of the others who volunteered as well. The truck took us to the main gate, where we were unloaded and shown into small barracks. Inside, SS men had each of us extend an arm where they etched the tattoo of a number. This number became the symbol for the Nazi concentration camp survivors. Our names and numbers were recorded in a record book.

After the SS man finished my tattoo, he read it back to me aloud, as if to say, "This is your name now."

"B6193," he announced in German.

I was so happy. I was so happy with the tattoo because I had done something that my father ordered me to do. And I was also happy because they would not have gone to the trouble of putting the numbers on us unless we were going to live outside of Auschwitz and do some kind of work. I was probably the happiest person in the room. I did not know what the next day might bring, but for that moment, I was happy.

They put us on a different truck, and we left this horrible place. The gates of Auschwitz-Birkenau clanked to a close behind us. We were so happy we wanted to jump for joy, but we didn't dare. Two SS guards sat in the back of the truck, and a bullet waited for us if we dared to stand. So we kept our joy in our stomachs.

We travelled for about two hours and ended up at a small labor camp in the middle of nowhere. It was "small" in comparison to Auschwitz, but it held about thirteen to fourteen hundred prisoners. The barracks were walking distance from a group of large factories where we would work. It almost seemed like we were being treated like normal human beings.

The factory produced anti-aircraft weapons for the German army. I was a kind of runner who ran around all day asking the civilian workmen what they needed. This might be a fresh supply of oil, a particular type of screw, or something like that.

Our coworkers were Polish, French, and Dutch. They seemed friendly enough but wouldn't talk to us or even to each other. If a Gestapo (German Secret State Police) or SS saw prisoners talk to each other, it would be a bullet for both of them. But a friendly smile exchanged between us young workers in passing was very welcome.

The first day I approached the Polish foreman I was assigned to. He immediately looked around for any SS or Gestapo. When he didn't see any, he stuck his finger out to signal that I should approach. It was very scary because I knew I was not supposed to talk to the civilians. But he told me to approach, so I did. He looked around again, then bent his head back down as if focused on his work. He said in Polish, "Tell your friends that the Russian army is very close by. You will be liberated very soon." An unbelievable hero! Why did he choose to tell me this? It was such a good feeling to hear something from a civilian. I could have cried with joy.

The next day when I came to him again to ask about his needs, he told me we had to talk in German. While he told me what he needed in German, at the same time he blinked at me, while nodding toward a nearby small garbage can.

In this short time, I learned a lot and understood that when he blinked he was conveying some kind of message, something he could not say out loud. When he finished telling me what he needed, I walked to the small garbage can, picked it up as if this was part of my job, and carried it outside where there was a bigger garbage can. I emptied the small can into the big one carefully, very carefully.

Sure enough, at the bottom of the small garbage can, I found a couple of bites of real Polish bread—with no sawdust. I couldn't believe it! I could not believe that this hero took such a grave risk and put himself in so much danger by passing up part of his meager meal so that he could share it with me!

I knew he could not throw away a larger portion. This was wartime. If he was caught putting half of his sandwich into the trash, he would have been shot.

The worst part was that I was unable to thank him. There were eyes and ears everywhere. If I spoke to him in Polish or told him thank you in German, it could have meant death for both of us.

To me, he was an unbelievable hero.

At this labor camp, I finally learned where the women, children, and elderly were sent when we first arrived at Auschwitz. About a month after we had arrived, a group of Hungarian prisoners was brought in from Auschwitz to replace prisoners who died or were killed. They shared the horrifying fact of what had been going on right in front of us. You already know—all the elderly, all the mothers, and all the small children who arrived there, just as my family did, were sent directly to those buildings emitting all the noxious smoke.

Those clouds of smoke with their ghastly odor came from gas chambers where prisoners were sent to be killed. My mother and baby brother and all the others were sent directly to the crematorium. The friends of my age were no more. This was how we found out about the crematoriums. My world was shaken. I broke out in sobs. Every single one of the boys around me cried.

The barracks echoed with the sounds of crying. We cried that day, and we cried that night. We cried every time we thought of our mothers, sisters, brothers, babies, and the elderly.

This unresolved anguish stayed with me and will be with me for the rest of my life whenever I think about the cruel death of my mother and my little brother, Gabi.

Nearly every day the SS or the Gestapo went through the factory and wrote down numbers. If a worker's tool broke, it might be considered sabotage, and so they wrote down the man's number. If you didn't meet your quota of work for the day, you would be part of the "entertainment" the next weekend.

Each Sunday the soldiers arranged benches and installed ropes with deadly nooses to create a row of gallows. We were rounded up and ordered to watch as several of the young and old were lined up. The soldiers prodded the victims to mount the benches, and the nooses were placed over their heads and around their throats. A sergeant read out the nature of the offense of each man. Then a couple of the SS, one on each side, kicked the benches away as the poor helpless men tried to speak a prayer. Their last words were lost in an eruption of shaking, gurgles, gasps, and screams that seemed never-ending but probably took no more than a minute or two.

It was so cruel that it's hard to explain. These men were savages. And we *had* to watch. If you bent down your head to avoid watching, the SS guards picked you up, and you were part of the following Sunday's activities. So we had to watch these horrible scenes while the SS stood in the background, drinking beer and laughing while they took pictures. *Unbelievable!* And we didn't understand why. Why would they kill the people who worked in the factories to help the Nazi war effort?

The only answer we ever got was from the Capos. They explained that it was for entertainment. The SS did this for weekend entertainment because during the week it's too boring in the factory. They had no one to shoot!

That ugly explanation made sense when we saw many of the SS take pictures, perhaps to send home and keep as souvenirs. Souvenirs to show their children when the war was over? I had seen such horrors already that little could still surprise me.

We began to notice unmistakable changes in the attitude of our captors, little signs that they were becoming uncertain, less aggressive, and less demanding.

On January 21, 1945, the group of factories where I worked became the target for enemy shelling.

Tomorrow we will be free, we thought. We traded brief secret smiles with each other.

Instead, the Capos ordered us to assemble outside. When all were accounted for, they shouted orders for us to march. We were frigid and shaking in our wooden shoes from the cold, wearing only our thin uniforms made of that mystery material in midwinter. We later learned that we marched in the coldest winter in recorded European history.

They kept us marching in that unbelievable cold from morning to midday to nightfall and on into the darkness. The SS bundled up with all kinds of warm clothing that left them sweating while we struggled along, afraid not to keep up.

Frostbite in my left foot led to the loss of a small piece of flesh on my big toe. I suffered with every step I took but somehow managed to keep going. The choice of "march or die" is a great incentive.

When we finally stopped for the night, we were each given two pieces of bread and told it was all we would get for the next two days. Normal people would eat it a little at a time. But we had no pockets, and so the only place to hide the bread was inside our shirts. A lot of famished men would be watching, forcing themselves to stay awake until someone fell asleep, and they could steal the bread. We had become animals, willing to steal from our own kind to stay alive.

We arrived at the train station and were loaded into boxcars, finally relieved from walking through that frightful weather. Before long the sounds of coughing and sneezing came from every part of the boxcar. It sounded as if a lot of people came down with a very bad cold. In time, I found out it wasn't a mere cold. We were saturated with lice, and lice carried the illness called typhus fever. People who lived through such terror and horror, now so close to what we knew must be the end of the war, died all around us. We traveled with dead bodies. We didn't throw their bodies out of the boxcar. They were our friends. Instead, we made a pile of the dead in one corner of the car.

When the train stopped, we were unloaded and marched a distance to what we learned was the Mauthausen-Gusen concentration camp in Austria. In an era of savage cruelty, this place would come to be known as one of the worst hells mankind has ever conceived.

An announcement was made that we must all go to the showers. This was a death sentence. All of us knew "the showers" was Nazi doublespeak for the gas chambers.

This time it really meant a shower of cold water to scrub off the caked dirt we had all collected on the three day journey. The promise of getting clean would have been more welcome if we had not been so desperate for sleep. Sleep that was not on a bone-chilling bed of snow.

While we showered, an announcement was called out for all the Capos in our group, the Capos who had been such a terror for us at the factory, to raise their hands. Instantly, hands shot in the air. Each of those cruel men undoubtedly expected to be called forward and restored to his position of authority.

We witnessed a horrible, hideous scene instead. I never thought it would be possible to have feelings about the fate of a Capo after all the unspeakably cruel things we experienced at their hands. But now the tables were turned. Apparently the Capos of Mauthausen feared they might lose their status and privileges to the newly arrived Capos in our group. They were prepared and dived into their self-assigned task with venom. With wooden clubs, they attacked each man who had raised his hand, one by one clubbing him to death. Blood, flesh, and bones were scattered everywhere.

After the terrors we had endured, *this* was the most vicious thing anyone could imagine.

I can still hear the cries and see the blood spurting. Merely writing this brings back the sickening feelings I felt then.

We watched in terror, certain that as soon as they finished with the Capos, they would turn their clubs upon the rest of us.

But, no. Their only goal was to protect their own privileges by viciously getting rid of others they saw as possible competition.

When the clubbing ended, we were sent to carry what body pieces remained of the Capo victims outside and dump the new bodies on the pile—the ever-rising pile of the dead.

I wish that putting these words onto paper to describe this nightmarish scene would finally erase these images from my memory forever. If only that could be the reality.

The kind of grotesque mistreatment we received every day can turn decent people into savages. Many of the horrible acts that threatened us came not from our captors but from some of our fellow prisoners. The never-ending hunger and cruelty turned some of the boys into young monsters who grabbed the tiny bits of food that were all we had to eat from the smallest and the weakest. Clearly, some were not going to survive, and the most vulnerable became victims. Within two weeks, the deaths began.

In our barracks, no one wanted to sleep against the walls in wintertime. The barracks were unheated of course. It felt like sleeping outdoors in the Arctic at nighttime, and the worst was having to sleep up against one of the walls. The rest of us could sleep body to body, providing at least a little warmth. Some mornings, many of those who slept against the wall did not wake up again.

One night at bedtime, we pushed and shoved each other more than usual fighting over who would sleep against the walls. The German who was the "leader" of our barracks couldn't bring us to order, so he left and notified the SS.

The team that responded included one man every prisoner knew by sight and knew to avoid, a man so vicious he would later make it into the pages of many books about the Holocaust. We knew him as Sergeant Kaduk, and we knew he took pleasure in murdering Jews. It seemed as if he was playing a personal bitter game of thinking up new ways to make dying an even greater horror.

He ordered all of us to stand in formation outside on this freezing winter night. He ordered us not to move at all.

To survive, each of us had to find a moment when the team of soldiers looked in another direction. We raised one foot for just a few seconds. I know it doesn't seem possible that raising one foot off the frigid ground for a few seconds at a time could make such a big difference, but it did. It was the difference between falling over dead or surviving for at least a few minutes more.

If we stood there without secretly raising one foot and then the other, we would freeze and die. Raise a foot within sight of a soldier, and we were kicked, savagely kicked, sometimes to death.

We stood there playing this deadly game for what must have been an hour.

When we were finally told we could go back into our barracks, less than half of us survived Kaduk's deadly game. Friends, companions, and soul mates, who managed to survive these most savage of conditions for all these months, were suddenly gone.

We quickly discovered that returning to the barracks didn't mean the end of this torturous night. We had to fall into formation to warm up by doing exercises. I was always in the front row because I was short. Alongside me was Robert Wasserberger, a youngster who had become my dear friend, like a brother. I saw that he was very weak, almost ready to collapse. I whispered, "Grab my pants so you don't fall."

He did, and it gave him balance for a few moments.

Kaduk saw that I allowed another prisoner to support himself so he wouldn't collapse. To help a friend to survive was impermissible.

He came over and kicked me in the back so hard and with such tremendous force that I slammed into the wall.

I had no strength left. I collapsed in the worst pain I had ever felt.

My throat and nose were so full of blood that I could not catch my breath and knew the end had finally come, that it was at last my turn to die.

At that moment, as if the God I no longer believed in decided it was not my turn to die yet, Kaduk turned and walked out.

My friends poured water into my mouth. That revived me. I saw the face of death and returned to the living. I knew I was still alive when I saw their thin, miserable faces smiling at me. They were so happy they had saved my life.

The pain from that savage kick lingered; it was so severe that I could barely sleep at night.

Each morning the Capos woke us. Most mornings there were some who never woke up again. They died in their sleep at night. The Capos chose prisoners at random for the awful, too familiar chore of carrying the dead outside. I was fourteen years old, the youngest and smallest, but often called on to suffer the task of helping another boy carry the body of a friend who died overnight. It was tossed without ceremony or prayer onto the enormous heap of frozen dead bodies.

In February, hundreds of captured Russian soldiers were imprisoned in our camp. One night, we were awakened by a great commotion. The SS discovered a breakout. The Russians had managed to dig a trench under one wall of the camp. Some four hundred of them, including their general, clawed their way through the trench and escaped. Of course, we were secretly happy for them—and envious.

About two hundred were recaptured and marched back into the camp. They were lined up and ordered to strip naked. After a time, two fire trucks arrived, driven by members of the SS. They stopped in front of the freezing Russians, pulled out the hoses from the trucks, and on command doused the Russians with water. In the freezing cold weather, it took just a few minutes for the Russians to become an ice sculpture of death, a grotesque image I will never be able to get out of my mind.

It was a warning to the rest of us: this is what happens if you try to escape.

As Allied forces advanced toward Germany and crossed the borders, the Nazis ordered camp prisoners to be moved more deeply into the heart of the country. At Mauthausen, we were organized into groups of about two thousand and sent out to march once again.

Every hour, at least one of us collapsed, unable to continue, yielding to death. They were our friends, our soul mates, yet we could do nothing to help them, not even pause long enough to say the Kiddish, the prayer for the dead. Would any of us have said the prayer if we had the chance? Were there any among us who still believed in God? A loving God who could allow this epic tragedy?

It quickly became clear that our captors did not bring any food for us. We had to provide for ourselves, eating from garbage dumps and grabbing anything edible each time we crossed a farmer's field. After all we had been through, the march seemed almost tolerable. We would soon discover why history would record it as one of the "Death Marches."

On the third day, near Linz, we approached a wide bridge and saw a large army force coming toward us, a force made up of both German and Hungarian soldiers with a number of half-track vehicles carrying machine guns.

As one Hungarian unit passed us on the bridge, I could not resist. I saw a young soldier who looked barely old enough to be in the army and thought that being so young he might still have some human feeling. I said softly in Hungarian, "Dear soldier, I'm very, very hungry. Maybe you can spare a piece of bread?"

He answered, "You dirty Jew, you don't need no food. You're going to hell."

I wanted to reply, "We're going together!" But I was afraid he would shoot me.

When they passed, a friend said to me, "You're crazy! If they saw what you did, they would shoot you."

"When you're hungry enough," I answered, "you'll do anything."

Moments later, without warning or reason, the half-tracks opened their machine gun fire at us.

I dove for the ground, and others piled on top of me.

When it was over, those who were still alive pulled themselves up off the ground. I was finally able to stand up, alive and without a scratch. But hundreds in our group lay dead in every direction. After all the death and cruelty I had seen, I still found this unimaginable.

When the Germans marched by, our guards told us, "Take off the clothes from the dead, wipe up the blood on the bridge, and throw the bodies into the river." With tears in our eyes, we did as we were ordered.

Eventually those of us who survived the death march arrived at a concentration camp called Gunskirchen. Most of my closest friends died on the journey.

It didn't seem possible, but of all the nightmare places we had been, this place was far worse, an unspeakable hell. I felt it was a place we were brought to die. After the war, I learned that this camp had only been constructed months earlier, but in the short time it existed, more than fifteen thousand Jewish prisoners were brought here on forced death marches like ours.

We had to retrieve drinking water from drainage ditches, folding our hands into the shape of a cup. Food was rare and in such small quantity that many of us took to eating the bark from the camp's trees. Piles of dead bodies lay in every direction.

On Friday, May 4, 1945, we had only been in the camp a short time when we heard commands shouted over the loudspeakers to the German soldiers. They were to leave the camp immediately. They scampered down from the watchtowers, and they raced out of the buildings and *ran* to their barracks. They hastily changed into civilian clothes and rushed out of the camp, throwing down their machine guns.

Did we snatch up the machine guns and end the lives of our captors as they fled? No, not a single one of us. We all rushed to the camp kitchens to look for food. I managed to grab a loaf of bread, but then found I couldn't push my way out through the crowd trying to push in. I escaped by climbing onto the shoulders of a stranger and worming my way out through a window. I had enough to share with my friends, but the other prisoners saw my puffed out shirt and instantly knew what I was hiding. They tore my shirt from me, grabbing, grasping, and snarling; they left me with nothing. I understood. Starved to the point of being all but dead, none had any morality or kindness left. Starvation erases all morals.

I found two of my friends, and we set off, shedding our wooden shoes even though it meant going barefoot. As we walked through sunset and into the darkness of night, we suddenly heard shouts of "STOP" in English.

We stopped and discovered a team of three American soldiers. Americans! One of them spoke a little German and pointed out the direction we should walk. He warned us we had a long way to go. They gave us small packages, gesturing that they contained something to chew. We set off again, weeping with pleasure as we chomped on the first sweet taste we had known since the outbreak of the war.

In one small town, American soldiers gave clothing to survivors. We gladly stripped out of our prison outfits, which were filthy with lice. The Americans dropped our clothing into a fire.

We eventually came to a small airport where there were some American cargo planes. There was a commotion nearby. I looked over and saw a dozen or so Polish youngsters beating a man—a man I recognized as the vicious Sergeant Kaduk who had kicked me so savagely. I joined in and landed some good kicks.

An American soldier approached us and fired a bullet into the air to scare us off. The others scrambled away, but I stayed. I struggled to make the soldier understand that this man was an SS sergeant. My anger made him suspicious, and he ripped away the sleeve of Kaduk's shirt, revealing a tattoo at his armpit. It was the emblem of the SS that this savage had once been so proud of.

Kaduk was terrified. He begged the soldier not to shoot him. I remember he said, "Don't shoot! I just followed orders."

The American didn't care what Kaduk had to say, nor did he hesitate. He raised his rifle and fired a bullet into Kaduk's head.

There could be no payback for what we had all been through, but I was so happy to see this murderer go to hell. I hugged the American and thanked him.

The following morning I was picked up by a truck of soldiers who were looking for the sick and injured. They took me and others to a hospital run by the American army open to all survivors. What a remarkable and wonderful thing! What a difference from the vicious tyrants who had been our captors.

I walked in and saw beds with clean white sheets that looked like a dream. I found an empty bed and let myself collapse onto it. When I woke, they told me I had been lying there for two days. A doctor examined me, and the army nurses who looked after me were gentle and caring.

I was hardly able to believe this miraculous change in my life. Yes, I was severely ill, itching all over, and too weak to get out of bed to even use the toilet. But I was fed and attended to by doctors and nurses who clearly cared about me and would do all they could to make me comfortable to speed my recovery.

From a world of misery to a world of caring, it was as if I had been reborn into a totally different universe.

PART TWO

HIDEOUS HOMECOMING

Four weeks later, I finally woke up one morning without a fever, and the next day I was able to go to the bathroom by myself. Weak and alone, I was determined to return to my hometown. I knew the doctors would say I was not yet ready to leave, but I was desperate to reunite with my father and my brother.

I was barefoot and wore nothing but a hospital gown that didn't even reach my knees, and I was dangerously skinny. I got out of bed, grabbed a bag of chocolates as I walked down the corridor and was out the door before anyone noticed. I knew it was not smart, but I knew it was something I had to do.

All of the war prisoners I met in the hospital believed, like me, that they were street smart. No wonder. We survived while thousands upon thousands around us did not. It never even occurred to me that I might have problems finding my way home.

To this day, I cannot forgive myself for leaving that hospital without showering thank yous to every gentle, caring American doctor and German nurse who saved my life.

But what now? I left the hospital with no clothes and had no means of travel. I couldn't walk from Germany to my hometown in Slovakia. About a block from the hospital, I chose a house at random, walked up the path, and knocked. After a few moments, a lady of perhaps thirty answered the door.

From my bone thin body and my limited German, she must have understood that I was from one of the camps. She invited me in and left. She came back moments later with a shirt, trousers, and shoes. She seemed to understand I didn't want pity or a fuss made. The trousers were too long, so she brought in a pair of shears and cut them to a good length.

When she was done, I felt warm with gratitude—not just for the clothes but for her generosity and willingness to help a young boy in need. I presented to her the bag of chocolates, keeping only a couple for myself. The gift made her happy, and I was repaid with a warm, appreciative smile.

On my way out, she pointed me to the train station where the American army had set up an office. At the army post, an interpreter translated for me while a young soldier in a small booth filled out a paper that identified me as a survivor. He shoved the papers and a pen toward me to sign. I picked up the pen, but my hand shook so badly that it was impossible to sign. He reached out, took my hand, and guided me in making some unreadable marks on the paper, marks that would be a substitute for my signature. I saw that he was crying; his tears trickled down his face. I wanted to hug him. If he had not been confined to that little booth, I would've put my arms around him and wrapped him in a warm, appreciative hug. Danke schön, German for thank you very much, didn't even come close to articulating the depth of my appreciation.

It took four or five hours before my train finally pulled into the station. I boarded the train for home. I felt exhilarated yet frightened. I didn't know what I would find. After an hour or two, the train stopped, and the conductor made an announcement. Everyone gathered their belongings and climbed off the train.

I didn't know that the bridges had all been bombed or destroyed in what I suppose was a last ditch effort to slow the advancing Allied forces. At each river, all passengers had to get out, wade across, and board another train on the other side. For me, the wading was like entertainment. I had little memory of fun; this was the closest to fun I had known since the army arrived in our town.

On the next train, I noticed a young man, a soldier, wearing a uniform I had never seen and looking at me as if he knew me. He got up, approached, and asked in German, "Where are you from?" I thought he meant what camp and told him the name of the camps I had been in.

"No, where are you from here in Europe?"

"Slovakia," I told him.

He bent down and hugged me. "I am from Slovakia also."

I almost started to cry when I saw a patch on his sleeve—a gold Star of David, the Jewish symbol.

"Why do you wear that," I asked.

He told me, "I am from Palestine, in the Jewish Brigade of the English army."

The army of England had a Jewish Brigade? I could hardly believe it.

His train stop came up, and he gave me all the food in his pouches. "You'll go home and get well, and maybe one day you'll serve like me in the army of Palestine." Then, he hugged me. It felt like heaven, such a wonderful feeling to be hugged by a Jewish soldier! Once again I was in tears. Once again they were tears of pleasure. I wanted to call out to everyone on our train car, "He's a Jewish soldier!" The train pulled into the station, and he got off. That brief encounter changed me. It gave me some sense of security—and the sense that a future was possible.

For me, there were still many hours of travel ahead. What had been a five-hour trip before the war, now took six days. When the last of the trains arrived in my hometown of Levice, there were people at the station to greet and help refugees like me. They directed me to a house in town, a large house set up by an American Jewish organization for survivors like me.

Still suffering from the typhus and even weaker after the journey, I must have looked a pathetic figure. A boy of fourteen should have weighed around one hundred pounds. I weighed barely more than half that.

The place I was taken to turned out to be both a blessing and a misery. A misery because we all suffered so badly during the war that living with other children who had been through similar experiences helped keep the unwanted memories alive. Yet being with these other survivors was a kind of miracle because only another survivor could understand what we had been through.

We needed each other to share, to hug, and to feel friendship. We became like a family, helping each other survive. I wanted only three meals a day, a warm bed, and gentle companions.

The house was large enough for some eighty survivors. For the months I lived there, I felt good during the day but cried myself to sleep at night. Most of us suffered from nightmares. I could not tell which was worse, my own nightmares or being awakened by the nightmares and cries of others.

At the beginning, I found life at the home to be boring. During the day, we were alone with no adults to help or assist us. After breakfast, we played card games, talked, or kept ourselves busy in some other ways until lunch. In the afternoon, volunteers sometimes loaded us onto a bus and took us to a playground or some not very interesting site. After dinner, people from town sometimes came to visit. They told of a trip they had taken, a book they had read, or maybe read to us from a newspaper or magazine. They may not have been very good entertainers, but there was a friendly, happy feeling. And "happy" was not a word any of us had recent experience with.

Try to imagine yourself at age fourteen with no parents, no siblings, and no grandparents. No one but a worn-out, bitter aunt who survived the Budapest ghetto. She worked at the home as a cook, and she tried to befriend me. Before the war, she and my family had not been close. Now she wanted to offer help. I felt like her efforts came from feeling sorry for me. Looking back, I suppose I should have allowed her efforts, even been grateful. But I didn't want pity. I evaded her as best I could.

Aside from her, I was the only survivor out of thirty-nine family members. I asked all over town about my family and my relatives. No one knew anything of them.

The days were occupied and tolerable. The terrors came at bedtime. Crying and tears were my bedtime companions. I tried everything I could think of. Nothing could keep me from crying myself to sleep night after night. I came to dread the setting sun and the darkness that followed. I was racked by headaches, and my nights were mostly sleepless. But the worst was the nightmares—a parade of the horrors I had witnessed and the suffering I had endured. I would be gently awakened and told I had been screaming and crying out for my mother, my father, and my brothers.

In the home, I quickly adjusted to this new life with its everyday routines that distracted me from thoughts of the war years. I did, however, listen to the radio for hours hoping to hear a mention of my father, my mother, and my brothers. There was nothing.

I was a strange, lost soul, a child who didn't want help from anyone, not from old friends and not from this household of new companions. Many of the young people around me reached out to help each other. I didn't want their help. I didn't want anyone to feel sorry for me.

Miki, age 15, at the center for survivors in Levice, Czechoslovakia

I found a few of my pre-war Christian friends and unloaded some of my camp stories on them. The stories made them cry, which I couldn't stand. I began to cross the street when I saw one of them coming.

My constant nightmares included an especially painful one: in my sleep, I would search all over the same city that my parents lived in, but I couldn't find them. These nightmares plagued me in those post-war years and continued for the next twenty years.

I was nothing more than a wild, wild child, almost a savage, a young teenager painfully alone in the world. It should have been a joy to see that some of the older survivors in the group began to make boy-girl connections, eventually leading to several marriages. Most of those couples settled in Israel. I knew I should have felt happy for them, but it only seemed to make my loneliness all the more painful.

I asked everyone I met whether they knew my father or brother. At last I found a man who had been at Dachau. He told me, "I knew your father and your brother before the war, and I know how they died. About twelve kilometers from Dachau, there is a mass grave site. That is where they are buried." Hearing this was a great relief because the question I so desperately sought an answer to had finally been answered. But at the same time it was of course a curse. It put an end to my cherished hope that we would eventually find each other, giving me at least part of my family again.

When I finally learned the details of how my father's and brother's lives ended, the pain was unbearable. They had been working under horrendous conditions, slaving to build one of the many underground facilities Hitler ordered. The records say some five thousand imprisoned workers died on this one project alone, yet Popik father and son managed to survive. They were working hard labor under the most severe conditions, pouring subterranean concrete ten to twelve hours a day.

One day, at the end of their shift, instead of being marched back to their camp, they were diverted through a forest. German soldiers were waiting for them. The prisoners were mercilessly machine-gunned to extinction. This act of cowardly cruelty was carried out because the American army was advancing. My brother, my father, and their entire group of some fifteen hundred men were slaughtered one week before the Liberation.

A week later, when General George S. Patton's army arrived, they were told about the workers who were slaughtered there. The officer had his soldiers force the German civilians who lived in the neighboring towns to dig up their bodies and rebury them in a mass grave next to a Christian cemetery with a tombstone.

I learned part of their fate months later from a Hungarian newspaper. In their story about this murderous event, the article, quoting German sources, claimed that almost all of the prisoners buried at the site had died of heart attack. The Germans were still unwilling to admit the truth about this deplorable act.

For me, it was unbearable to learn how needlessly my father and brother died. I cried for days and broke out in tears many times in the months ahead, unable to stop playing out this scene in my head.

I was one of the youngest, one of the very, very few of my age to survive the worst of the camps. Confused and miserable, I was a difficult person. It did not help that people sometimes came to the house in hopes of finding information about their loved ones, just as I had asked every survivor I encountered about my brother and father. These desperate visitors came to the home hoping to finally find someone who could tell them anything about their parents or their children. On a few occasions, the person they asked about was someone I had known.

I was caught in the middle. What was worse? For me to say, "No, I never encountered him," or "Yes, I knew him," and see the look of misery when I confirmed the person was dead? And then I tried to avoid answering their questions about the manner of death. To answer that question was simply too gruesome.

Most of the girls in the home did factory work during the war. It's possible that some of them were sex slaves, girls who were selected to serve in brothels available to the SS guards. These girls were often raped by some twenty or more men in a single day. Of all the horrors I underwent or witnessed, the misery of these girls must have been vastly worse. I can only think that for anyone trapped in that way, death would have been a blessing.

As the months went by, I slowly became more stable. The nightmares continued, but my attitude gradually improved. I smile now when I remember that around the time I turned fifteen, I noticed the face staring back at me in the mirror looked a mess. My hair stood up in every direction, and for weeks no amount of brushing could tame it. My facial expression announced "unhappy" and "miserable."

I still remember discovering that I wanted to look more normal. I wanted to be *good looking*! I began the struggle to tame my hair. I began to plow through the items in the large storage room that was filled with used clothing to look for items my size that would make me look more respectable, more "everyday."

I began to long for remembrances of my family in the days before the war. Occasionally my path around town took me past our old house. I allowed myself that route out of what, curiosity? Longing? I turned onto the street knowing that just walking past the house was going to be painful, and it always was.

Eventually, I began to wonder about the people who had stepped up in the world by being given the ownership of a home that "a Jew family" had lived in and cherished for years before they were packed off to the camps. I began to have visions of the decorations I grew up with—the set of dishes we ate from, the art work, and the family pictures that hung on the walls or stood in frames on the tables.

One day, steeling myself, I went to the house and knocked on the door. An old man answered.

He confirmed that he and his family had lived in the house since the Jews were moved to the town ghetto. By chance did they still have any of the family pictures that had been left behind? I was told no. They sold some of the dishes and things and threw away everything else no one wanted.

He seemed to be afraid I was going to try to force them out and take the house away.

I left quickly and never went back.

Many years later, I learned that the house was torn down for low-income housing. It's far less painful to think of the family home I grew up in is no longer standing with strangers living in it.

THE BIRTH OF ISRAEL

After living at the survivors' home for about a year, I was still very confused. I didn't know where I was in life, and I felt I hadn't found my place. I also knew too well that the staff and many of the other survivors who lived there found me difficult. I often lashed out for no good reason. I started arguments over trivial things, and later I became annoyed when someone else started an argument over something just as trivial.

Then one day we were introduced to some men and women from Palestine, which was then still a territory under the control of the British.

These visitors visited homes like ours to talk to us about becoming settlers in what was soon to be the new state of Israel. For me, the timing was special. I was beginning to feel Jewish again, and these people talked about settling in the new Jewish homeland. "The state of Israel will be born again," they told us. I could feel the excitement and enthusiasm wafting through every corner of the room.

I was one of the first to sign up, but eventually most or all of the others added their names to the list. I could not escape my gnawing memories, but this new focus was a welcome distraction. More than that, it gave me a sense of commitment to something outside of my own personal selfish needs.

We moved out of the survivors' home to a residence in the town of Bratislava, the capital city of Slovakia, which is set on a hilltop overlooking the Danube River. In the months that followed, I worked half of the day in a factory, turning out nuts, bolts, and other small parts used to build machinery. For the remainder of the afternoon, we studied Hebrew, the benefits and challenges of life in Israel, the politics of the region, the anger in the Arab world, and the dangers that people might face living in the new Israel.

My education stopped just after my bar mitzvah. These months of afternoon classes for the child survivors were the only additional education I ever received in my lifetime.

Living in the Bratislava home, as with the home in Levice, was very difficult for me. This continued to be a confusing and painful period of my life. I was surrounded by survivors, but survivors who had no sense of what I had been through. None of them had ever been in Auschwitz, Mauthausen, or any other of the nightmare-on-earth hellholes where I witnessed one friend after another after another die a torturous death. Each one was a reminder that you might be next.

My companions at the Bratislava home survived the war in hiding or at worst, in concentration camps much less harsh and cruel than what I had witnessed and suffered. They did not have nightmares like mine. They could still laugh, sing, and play. I looked on as if standing on the sidewalk watching a party I was not invited to.

I lived as that unhappy outsider for about two years, until the day that Great Britain announced finally arrived. At midnight on May 14, 1948, the British Mandate officially terminated. A document called the "Declaration of the Establishment of the state of Israel" was proclaimed. The lands we now know as Israel became a separate nation recognized by the United Nations as independent and self-ruling.

We danced in the streets, danced and danced almost until morning. What struck me most of all was that it wasn't just Jews who celebrated. The streets were just as crowded with "goyim" (non-Jews) who danced, drank, and cheered with us. It was one of the most memorable nights of my life.

The next day, we learned that people all over Slovakia took to the streets just as we had.

Soon after, we were told to pack our clothes and get ready to leave. We loaded into trucks and were driven to a Displaced Persons camp in Germany. This was the first leg of our trip to what the Jewish people have always called, "The Promised Land." There all of us, the young women and young men, received military training to prepare us to serve in the army once we reached Israel. After about a month of training, we were driven to a remote site on the Mediterranean near the border of France and Italy. Everything was in secret. If the Egyptians found out our ship was sailing to Israel, they would send a warship to sink us.

We woke up the next morning and saw the boat that was to take us out to the ship we were to travel on anchored offshore. This short first leg was on an ancient wreck of a vessel that looked as if it might spring a leak and sink to the bottom of the sea at any moment.

We loaded onto the boat, all eight hundred of us, packed in so tight that it felt like you needed to be careful reaching into your pocket or your hand would end up in the pocket of the person next to you. Finally, the anchor was hauled in, and we were on our way. Some immediately felt seasick. Everybody else who was topside searched the horizon to be the first to spot the mother ship for our eleven day journey to Israel.

But there was no mother ship.

The vastly overcrowded boat to Israel, May 1948

This dilapidated, ready-to-fall-apart, pathetic vessel was our transport to the promised land. Fervent prayers were said every morning and every evening.

The first night, as soon as it was dark enough, I snuck up to the bow, where a lot of the food stock was stowed. I pulled open a large box of biscuits, stacked the contents onto the deck, and curled up in the empty box. It provided me with something no one else had, a place to sleep without a stranger crowded up against me on each side. A tough-looking, young man who saw me warned, "If the captain finds out, he'll kill you."

"I don't care," I told him. I was asleep within moments.

On the second night, my dear friend, Erno, begged for permission to share the box with me, and I agreed. We crowded in together every night for the rest of the voyage.

From the beginning, I never had much confidence this miserable excuse for a ship would actually make it all the way to Israel. But on the morning of our eleventh day, I woke up to a sight that generated unbelievable feelings within me and the others on board. We could see the mountains of Jerusalem. This was near the end of May 1948, one of the most memorable days of my life.

A feeling of high excitement swept the ship, some broke out in tears, and a number of men were so eager that they jumped overboard and tried to swim ashore. Boats pushed off from the docks and motored out to pick us up. As soon as we got ashore, we discovered that the buses waiting for us were stacked with wonderful Israeli oranges. Awash in unbelievably good feelings, it felt like coming home after a long, long, unhappy journey.

Families were loaded onto buses to go to kibbutzes (a collective community). Men and women who were not part of a family were loaded onto other buses and taken to a different kibbutz.

The lines outside the shower stalls required patience. Each man spent up to a half-hour trying to scrub off the dirt from the ship's engines that was caked onto our heads, faces, and every exposed body part.

When my turn finally came, I felt that washing off the grime was a symbol of washing off the past, marking the beginning of a new life.

After the first night of decent sleep since boarding the ship, we woke the next morning to find that uniforms had been laid out. Time to be soldiers to help the new state of Israel take over the mandated territories and make the area safe for the Jewish people.

Still in my teens and short for my age, I was surprised but pleased to be chosen for duty with a special group of fighters, the Palmach unit. Palmach is Hebrew for "strike force." It was the elite fighting force of the Haganah, the underground army, a unit so informal that the general sat down to eat breakfast every morning with the privates. I felt a great sense of privilege to be in the company of the young men, and yes, young women, who made up this elite force. Being taken in by this much admired unit made me feel very special. I confess that when off duty and spending time with the local young citizens, I was so proud I was a bit of a show-off. Everyone knew what the Palmach was. People looked at me with appreciation and respect. I thrived on the admiration.

Miki as a soldier in the Palmach, 1948

The Palmach called for great courage. I quickly found out why I, as a scrawny seventeen-year-old, was selected to serve with them. The Israelis had discovered that the young were best suited for this unit. They had learned that a man with a wife and maybe a child or two has a sense of responsibility and so was more concerned with his own safety. When you're young and unattached, you don't think about the danger. In the months ahead, I never once feared that I might be wounded or killed.

At the end of our brief three week training, I knew how to load, fire, and clean my rifle, as well as other basic soldier tactics. I was sent to join a unit with eight other Palmach soldiers, who were part of the force focused on gaining control of Jerusalem. I also learned about the rules concerning drinking. We couldn't. Israeli soldiers were not allowed to drink, making the Israeli army probably the only armed force in the world with this rule. But for us, the enemy was always close at hand. We never knew when shooting might begin. The rule made good sense.

We transported water and flour to the besieged city of Jerusalem, slipping past soldiers of the Jordanian army. Arabs were all around, and there were so few of us. Yet it felt like an adventure. We felt a sense of freedom, dignity, and pride in fighting to help launch Israel, the new Jewish state.

I never felt any fear either because I was so young or so naïve. I was proud to fight to recover the land that Moses had led his people to. I carried a secure sense and a boyish confidence that no bullet would ever find me. When I was shot at, I stood up at my full height unafraid to make myself an easy target as I shot back.

After two months with my unit, an Arab bullet hit my right leg, passing straight through the flesh and out the other side without damaging a bone. Incredibly, I was in the hospital for only three days and rejoined my unit with barely any pain from the wound.

When pain did come, it was from an unexpected source. One night as I prepared for sleep, I felt agony in my back, so bad that I could barely move. They took me to a hospital in Jerusalem, where a doctor examined me, asked some questions, and then explained that my right kidney had been destroyed. Of course, I knew how—it was from the kick by the savage SS sergeant Kaduk.

The doctor told me, "You are very lucky." He said that we are born with two kidneys, and some people who lose one are able to live the rest of their lives with just the one healthy kidney. "If you've lived this long on only one kidney, you don't have anything to worry about as far as kidneys are concerned," he said.

So I'm here, and the monster from Mauthausen is not. It pleases me to think that his family probably never found out what happened to him.

I was back on duty and wounded again from taking shrapnel in my hand that left me in pain for years. Strangely the wounds made me proud, even happy. Given leave, I was treated like a hero. Everyone knew I was part of the highly respected Palmach. I was back on duty after only twenty-four hours.

After a year, I was transferred to the regular Israeli army and promoted to sergeant in an armored truck unit.

Young soldiers like me were required to serve two years in the army. The day came when I was told to pack my gear and board a truck to be taken to the discharge center. The others I arrived with were given their discharges within two days but not me. Each day I was told some version of, "We aren't able to release you yet."

Finally, I insisted on speaking with the officer in charge. I was ushered in to see him, and he studied my papers. In the event Israel called soldiers back to active duty, they needed to know where to reach me. On my form, I left the "HOME ADDRESS" line blank, since I didn't have any family and didn't know where I was going to live. I explained my situation. The officer was sympathetic. He wrote something on my form and called for the sergeant, who came in and looked at the form.

He said to the officer, "But, sir, that's *your* address."

"Yes," he said. "He'll let me know when he has found a place to live."

With that, I was no longer on active military duty. My next challenge was to find a place to live and a job to earn my keep.

In Haifa, I happily ran into Erno, my dear friend who had shared the box-as-a-bed with me on the ship to Israel. He said he was happy to let me share his room in a house that had been captured from the Arabs, but he wasn't able to help me find a job. He had had no success on his own job-hunt. We tracked down some of our army buddies and found they were no better off. Desperate, a few of us took work unloading cargo ships at night. It was laborious, all-brawn-no-brain work that paid so little we could barely afford to buy food. Some other ex-soldiers working on the docks told us about a "game" they invented, which we quickly adopted. Once or twice a shift when we'd spot a crate marked as containing some tempting kind of food stuffs, we signaled the crane operator and then loaded the box onto the crane so it fell off while being moved from ship to pier. We each took a share of the bounty and then sold the rest.

None of us claimed to be saints, just hungry. Hungry ex-soldiers who had served our new country but had no skills or talents to earn a decent living.

This all came to an end one night with one of our regular "accidents," this one a crate of sardines. It just so happened that one of our bosses came onto the dock just as we stuffed our pockets with the sardine cans. The whole pack of us was fired.

I was looking for new work and happened to spot a truck driven by a former army friend. I flagged him down, and we chatted and caught up on the usual things. I told him, "I need your help finding a job." He said he worked for the Weitzman Institute, and that they had contracts with some drilling companies to find sources of water and sources of oil. So I went to one of the companies.

The man I met with was a rough-looking, tough guy from Poland. When I told him I was looking for a job, he answered, "Are you crazy? It's terrible work. Look at my hands." His hands were like claws and covered with ugly callouses.

I told him, "I'm a survivor of the Nazi camps. My parents are dead, and my entire family is dead with the exception of my old aunt. I need work. I'll do anything."

It was as if he was suddenly struck by lightening. He got up, came around the desk, and hugged me. He was almost in tears.

He called out, and another man came in. My interviewer snapped at him, "Find this boy a job, today! Right now."

I started later that very same day outside Tel Aviv on the night shift with a crew drilling for water. It was tough work, just as the man warned me, but I didn't care. We drilled deep into the earth, pulled up the soil, and checked it for viscosity to reveal the presence of water or oil.

It was dangerous work perhaps, but it doesn't take much brainpower. After a few hours on that first shift, I knew all that I needed to know.

The big surprise was when payday came. I discovered this rough work paid as much in a week as my friends earned in a month.

In time, I discovered I was a natural leader. Within six to eight months, I learned as much as I needed to become an experienced driller.

This led to a new job, working for a private company that was drilling all over Israel looking for water and oil. The work demanded rough physical labor, but I already knew that suited me. Those years in the camps turned me into a fighter. I was ready to take on whatever battles I might face in the struggle to survive and succeed.

Within four years I became the rig manager of a drilling crew.

Deepwater drilling in Negev Desert, Israel, 1952

One weekend I went out with some friends, and I met a girl named Esther who worked in a cigarette factory. I found out later that she had seen a picture of me and announced she wanted to be introduced. She was Russian, and quite young, only sixteen. I had already turned twenty. But she was good looking and very, very smart. Though she had hardly any schooling, she knew all the Russian literary classics. I soon discovered that older friends came to her for advice. Though young, she was wise about life. She was lively and good company, and the centerpiece in any crowd.

Her childhood had been difficult. At age five in Russia, she had been run over by a horse-drawn carriage. A Jewish doctor took her under his care, but his hospital was far away from where her parents lived. They had little money, and so she spent the next seven years under the doctor's care, never once seeing her parents. When she finally rejoined her parents as a teenager, the family moved to Palestine, but the three could barely communicate. For Esther, at the hospital and in the local school, the only language was Russian. Her parents, who spoke Yiddish, knew virtually no Russian.

When she and I met, her limp was barely noticeable. We were drawn to each other from the start. Soon we spent entire evenings together, at first with friends and then just the two of us. We went to movies together and went dancing. Dating! This was a new world for me.

Her mother was not exactly crazy about me. I was making good money, but I was very poor. Worse, I still had not recovered my belief in God and would not attend services. And, on top of that, she witnessed my split personality. I was usually friendly, but I exploded in outbursts of anger at times. My painful memories and the frequent haunting nightmares that continued to plague me had turned me into a difficult man.

After five months, I knew I wanted Esther for my wife. Despite my too frequent outbursts, her mother and father gave us a nice wedding.

One day not long after, Esther and I were out for a stroll when a passing convertible suddenly pulled to a halt. The driver jumped out and ran toward me shouting greetings. I could hardly believe it. It was my dear friend Robert Wasserberger from the concentration camps. We hugged, patted each other, and practically cried. We all but danced with pleasure at this unlikely and totally unexpected reunion. For all of us, there are some people we encounter along the way and experience a special connection that is lasting and unforgettable.

We introduced our wives and stood there on the street for what must have been half an hour, catching each other up. It was the revival of a special kind of friendship, the kind that can only be understood by people who survived what he and I had both been through.

A few months after our encounter, Esther gave birth to our first child. We named her "Frida," in memory of my mother.

Esther's mother held the infant up to me and said, "You see, look at her. There is a God." I looked and saw the miracle that is newborn life and recognized I might have just taken the first step toward recovering my belief in God.

As I recount this, there are tears in my eyes.

My mother-in-law continued, "Next Yom Kippur, you will go to temple." She had chosen the holiest day in the Jewish calendar, the time when you atone for the sins you committed against God in the past year.

I went, and though still angry with God, it proved to be the first step in the slow, slow return of my belief.

DRILLING IN FRANCE,
SIDETRACKED IN MEXICO

One of the sad jokes among Jews everywhere is that Moses led his followers to settle in the only part of the Middle East where there is almost no oil. In 1958, the Israeli drilling company I worked for gave up the search and decided to focus exclusively on the search for additional sources of water. At about the same time, the company landed a deal to send crews and equipment to France, where new oil had been discovered. They wanted me to be part of the package based on my experience as a seasoned team leader. When I first heard the offer, I took it as a great honor and pleasure. I had long admired the French, and the salary they offered was excellent. It seemed a once-in-a-lifetime opportunity. Esther agreed it was too good to turn down.

Yet the idea of leaving Israel was very hard, almost like being torn away from my family once again—a "family" that included other war survivors and the Israelis we had come to feel so close to. Even so, with our daughter Frida, then age five, we set out on a journey that eventually took us to our new residence in the southwest of France, the town of Pontenx-les-Forges.

We found a place for rent, a floor in the home of a local family. The negotiations were a bit difficult. We had to find an interpreter since they spoke little English, and we spoke no French.

Once we settled in, we placed Frida in kindergarten and found she learned French faster than Esther and I. Within three or four months, she spoke French almost like a native.

The people of the town were friendly. Our being Jewish seemed to make no difference to them. We never experienced any animosity or anti-Semitism, and we became friends with some of the local families. We went on family trips together and loved to let them show off their colorful and charming country to us.

You might wonder how I could be the leader of a drilling team, when my crew was all French, and I didn't speak their language. Roughnecks, the term for basic-level oil field workers, already know the process. In any case, a drilling site is too noisy to shout orders, so most of the time, a hand-signal is enough. And it didn't take me long to learn the French terms for the orders I needed to give.

There's also an advantage to using a different language. When the crew did something wrong and in my concern I'd yell at them, they were able to discern my anger well enough to address the problem. But if I called them stupid, careless, clumsy, or whatever, they couldn't understand me. So they couldn't hold a grudge because they didn't know what names I had called them.

The busy days kept me focused on the present, but there were too many nights where I still trembled and cried out from those inerasable memories. I was difficult to live with, had terrible nightmares, and too often exploded over small issues. Esther suffered at witnessing my struggles. She developed techniques to calm me down, demonstrating more patience and tolerance than perhaps I deserved.

We didn't find oil in Pontenx-les-Forges, but we did find natural gas, which earned us much praise. Over the next two years, we drilled in one site after another, and so we lived in five different French villages. We found oil once in a village outside Paris near the Orly airport.

When we first arrived in that village, we discovered a problem. The only local school in town was a Christian school. I explained the situation to Frida, and she didn't have a problem with it, nor did the bubbly religious teachers. We quickly discovered that Frida was comfortable with the situation, well treated, and popular with the other students.

Esther and I both came to love France and the French people, but there were no Jewish families or synagogues nearby. The time had come to move, and the United States was at the top of the list. First, we arranged to stop in Mexico where Esther's mother, Hinda, lived. Mother and daughter had not seen each other for three years, so an extended visit was due.

We arrived in Mexico City in early 1960 and settled into an apartment

Hinda found for us in the same building where she lived.

Hinda earned a good income as a kind of inspector who ensured that the food served in Jewish restaurants and synagogues met the stringent requirements of Orthodox Jews. She was highly regarded in the Jewish community and had many friends. But I soon found Mexico did not please me, especially not after France. Mexico City in those days was largely a slum, and a place where working men were paid so little that it was understood they would steal whatever they could to feed their families. To get any service or assistance from the government, you had to pay a bribe.

As French speakers, Esther and I, as well as eight-year-old Frida, picked up Spanish rather easily, yet I couldn't find work. Finally, a man Hinda knew, a Zionist who wanted to help, gave me a job in his factory where they manufactured jukeboxes, coin-operated music machines used in restaurants and bars that let patrons pick the songs they want to hear or dance to.

Maybe saying he gave me a "job" isn't quite the right term. At first, I did almost nothing but sit around. The pay reflected what I was worth to his business; it wasn't even enough to pay our rent. But after six or seven months, the owner made me one of what they called the "confidence men," a man he could trust, so I was promoted to doing some of the buying for the company.

Our plan to stopover for just a few months was turned upside down when Esther found she was pregnant again. I was torn emotionally, delighted that we were adding another member to our little family and yet haunted at thoughts of staying in Mexico longer.

When baby Anita arrived at the beginning of December 1960, Esther and Hinda turned on the pressure about not taking an infant to a new country where we didn't know anyone or even have a place to live. With my uncomfortable work situation in Mexico, the idea of staying longer disturbed me, but it was certainly better for Esther and our new baby. I agreed we would stay in Mexico for a time.

Finally, when Anita was a little over two, I announced that it was time to move on. This "brief" stopover had been stretched into nearly three years. My mother-in-law, of course, would have been elated if we chose to settle in Mexico. She tried to convince us to stay, insisting that Mexico was "a golden land, a beautiful country, and in time you will become rich."

I could not be swayed. Aside from America, we only ever considered living in Israel, but they gave up seeking oil, the only work I knew. I decided I would take a trip to Texas, the crude oil capital of the United States, and search for a job.

Shortly after New Years of 1963, I packed a bag and left on a job hunting trip to Houston. As soon as I checked into a small hotel, I went out to explore the city. What I saw lived up to all I had heard about big cities in America. It was modern, clean, with beautiful tall buildings stretching skyward, one after another. In downtown Houston, it seemed to me that most of the people walked with purpose, as if on their way to make important decisions or take important actions. They were well dressed with the ladies in full makeup and styled hair.

I also discovered an ugly side to Houston. One day, I stood at a bus stop and bought a Coke from a black woman. I noticed people staring at me as if I had done something unacceptable. The bus came, and I boarded and sat down next to a black man. Again, I received stares of disapproval. Many of the passengers turned to stare at me. Was I imagining this, or was I seeing real prejudice?

Esther holding baby Anita and Frida in Acapulco, 1962

I knew too well the bitterness and sour taste of racial hatred. It made me sad to think this could exist in America. And if real, it shocked me to wonder if this was just a dark feature of Houston, or was all of Texas like this? Worse, was it this way all over the United States?

On Friday evening, I went to a Houston reform temple. After the service, I played dumb and hung around to listen for men who spoke Yiddish. I joined in on one conversation and said in Yiddish, "I'm from Israel looking for a job in the oil fields."

Finally, one man said, "Wait here." He came back in minutes with a piece of paper and told me, "Monday, go see this man."

I treated myself to a good dinner and enjoyed the babble of English, occasional laughter, and the overall sense people were relaxing and having a good time.

Monday morning I called the man whose name I had been given and was put on his calendar for the same afternoon. I found him in an elegant, impressive office, behind a large desk. He was a big guy built like President Lyndon Johnson. I told him I was a Holocaust survivor and had become a driller in Israel. He said this company in its early days had sent some people there to teach the Israelis drilling techniques. When he heard that I worked in France as a driller in charge of a crew and that I had nine years of experience, it was enough to seal the deal. He gave me papers that said I was hired.

I walked out in love with America, in love with the company, and eager to share my news with Esther. I rejoined my family pleased and proud I found a job at a very handsome salary. When I shared the news, the family cried together in pleasure and happiness with dreams of a prosperous, glowing, new life.

At the U.S. Consulate in Mexico City, we filled out the forms for the green cards that would allow the four of us to enter the United States.

We packed and said our goodbyes, but the happiness did not last. Before our green cards were even ready to pick up, I received word from the oil company that the job they had for me was not full-time and would be only ten days a month.

The painful truth was that I had shown up at a distressing time for the U.S. oil industry. The Arab countries were pumping so much oil that the world oil prices had collapsed. U.S. oil companies were barely able to make a profit. They drastically cut back production, pumping barely more than enough to keep the machinery from deteriorating. Sadly, working only ten days a month would not provide enough for us to live on.

Conversations with friends in Mexico about my situation eventually led to one of those encounters that brighten a person's life. One day I was introduced to a man who gave me an odd handshake. It turned out he mistook me for a member of his Masonic Temple and gave me the handshake Masons use with each other. We got into a conversation, and when he heard about my background and my job-hunting, he said, "You're a driller? I have a good friend in Long Beach who'll get you a job."

Where was this mysterious Long Beach?

His answer surprised me. "It's part of Los Angeles."

I always thought Los Angeles sounded like one of the most vibrant and exciting cities in America. The idea of us settling there made me smile every time I thought about it.

I talked it out with Esther and reassured her. She knew that money would not be an issue. We sold our last apartment in France. That income plus what we had saved every month from my salary meant we had the equivalent of some $12,000 American dollars. It felt like enough to make us feel free of money problems.

A different wife in these circumstances might not have been happy that her husband was leaving the family behind, but it was only temporary. We would soon be together in the United States of America.

Three days later, I was on a Greyhound bus from Mexico City to Los Angeles.

When the bus arrived at the border and all the passengers passed questioning and the baggage search, we reboarded the bus and headed north onto the highway. I passed through the border into the United States for the first time. I was no longer a visitor but one of the people of the nation. There was a smile on my face, the closest I would get to tears of joy.

The Greyhound bus terminal in Los Angeles back then was not in the best part of downtown. I got off the bus, picked up my bag, and just started walking. I wanted to feel excited and impressed but instead felt strangely disappointed. There was nothing beautiful about the buildings, and the people didn't seem alive with purpose or thriving with success.

In a couple of blocks, I came to a hotel, went in, and booked a room. The room they gave me was disgusting. The walls were soaking wet, and the room was filthy. This was not an encouraging introduction to the country of wealth and beauty I had seen in movies, heard about, and dreamed about for so long. I checked out the next morning and found another place, the Hotel Cecil. I did not know about this hotel's reputation. It turns out bodies have been found there. It has been a hiding place for murderers and has a reputation for being haunted.

The next day, walking the streets, I ran into an Israeli I knew from Mexico City. Just talking to him lifted my spirits. When I told him where I was staying, he said, "Jewish people don't stay in downtown. Take a bus and go to the Fairfax neighborhood. It's full of Israelis."

I went to the Fairfax district and wandered around a little. I felt lost and uncertain but at the same time comfortable to be in a place that felt a little like Israel with people speaking a language I understood. After France and Mexico, this felt a little like coming home. I didn't really know what to expect of Los Angeles, but I began to think that it might be the best of all possible choices.

In those days, Fairfax was like a Jewish ghetto, filled with survivors and with settlers from Israel. The streets were crowded with busy housewives chattering and calling out in Hebrew and Yiddish. Everybody seemed to know everybody else, and the streets were filled with Jewish delis, bakeshops, and cleaners. The sidewalks were busy with Jewish housewives, and Jewish old ladies hurried by with their shopping baskets. I laugh now thinking about the good feelings it all brought me, how young it made me feel, and how happy I was to be with people like me, people I could relate to. Yes, I knew this wasn't what all of America was like, but I felt at home on these streets and at home among these people.

I walked around, and I met a couple of young Israelis. One seemed like a bum but later became well known as the founder of Jerry's Deli, a favorite Los Angeles hangout, and the other had a job in a sausage factory. The two shared a small apartment in the Fairfax area. It had an extra bedroom, and they invited me to move in with them.

The next day, I found my way to a part of Los Angeles called Signal Hill. This is a surprise and wonder to many people. Right within the city limits of Los Angeles, there were oilfields with the familiar oil-drilling rigs visibly pumping away. Even more surprising, those same oilfields are there today still pumping oil. There is even an operating well on the grounds of Beverly Hills High School. But I think they are ashamed of this one. It's covered over with paneling painted with flowers! This well has been operating for a century and is said to produce some 400 barrels a day. In Beverly Hills!

It's amazing to me that there seems to be oil almost everywhere around the globe. Though much of it is too deep to reach with today's technology, we still recover quantities almost too great to imagine around the world every day. All as if God, if there is one, had been thinking ahead to provide gas for our cars, heating, and a major ingredient for plastics, chemicals, and a vast variety of products we use every day.

I needed to take three different buses to get to the office of the man I was to referred to by my friend in Mexico. The walls were decorated with pictures of Arabs in elaborate gowns and headpieces. The man who interviewed me showed little interest. It was obvious he wasn't impressed. I suppose he was used to hiring big, sturdy, and strong oilfield workers, and here I was, young and skinny, not what most roughnecks and drillers look like. And I spoke very little English.

He asked questions about my experience. Did he believe I had led drilling teams in Israel and in France? Maybe. Maybe not.

He said he would talk to his boss and call me. A week went by. Two weeks. Still, no call. I looked up other oil companies in the telephone directory, made appointments, rented a car, and drove to various parts of the city. Could my poor English make a difference? That never occurred to me. All around Los Angeles I found myself with people who didn't speak English well. They all seemed to have jobs. And the language I needed in the oilfield, I already knew. In the oilfields, the language was universal. So it wasn't the language problem that kept me from landing a job.

I asked my roommates what they thought I could do. They told me I should go ask for work at a Jewish agency that helped people find jobs. I went, and they put me in touch with a man who laid carpets and needed another crewman. Heaven have pity on me. I never laid carpets in my life. But I went to meet the carpet man, and he put me to work. This was a crazy guy. He worked so fast it was like he had a windstorm at his back. He banged his hammer so hard and moved down the line so fast, I couldn't believe it. He was practically a blur.

I started on a Thursday and worked through Friday. At the end of Friday, he handed me and the other helper each an envelope. We walked out together, and he spoke to me in Yiddish. This was more than a little surprising; he was a black man.

"Where did you learn Yiddish," I asked.

He said, "I've been working with Jewish people all my life."

I thought to myself, "A black guy that speaks Yiddish. This is good."

When I got to the apartment and opened the envelope, I fainted. I actually fainted. My pay for two days of work was $16.40.

I never returned to that job.

I woke up every morning and thought, "Maybe today I will get a call from the oil company." They never called, and they never wrote. This is the kind of disappointment that rips at the soul. The American dream was turning out to be a nightmare. I later told Esther we made a mistake in leaving France. We had a good life there and good friends. I could have found another job in the oil fields.

My roommates suggested another possibility. They knew a Polish man who did house painting. I went to see him, and he said I was hired. Glad as I was to find another job, my new boss was worse than the first one by far, probably the most unpleasant man I had met since the Nazis. Cheap and mean, he was determined we spend no longer than a single day on each house. It was hard work, but the hardest part was learning that working for such a person can stir up hateful feelings and destroy your spirit. Still, it paid twice as much as the carpeting at $32 a day.

After two weeks, I found a furnished one bedroom apartment in a fairly new building, renting for only $100 a month. The place was small but clean and nice enough. I called Esther and told her to pack up, buy airplane tickets for herself and the girls, and come join me. For our close little family, it felt like we had been apart a long time.

Happy as I was at the thought of having them with me again, I was also anxious about how they would respond to Los Angeles, America, and Americans.

PART THREE

AMERICANS AT LAST

My family flew into Los Angeles in June. This was the longest time we had ever been apart, and I had missed them terribly. Esther was almost in tears, but now we were together and in America at last. All the loneliness I had felt washed away.

When we arrived to our little apartment in Fairfax, they were pleased and adapted readily. They never complained about the one bedroom. What didn't go over so well was my work as a house painter instead of drilling in the oilfields. It wasn't just the job or the working conditions. One day I made the mistake of bringing my lunch bag home. Esther demanded, "How come you didn't finish your sandwiches?"

Without stopping to think, I answered honestly, "He wouldn't let me." She insisted that I give her my boss's phone number. She called, gave her name, and said, "My husband is working for you?" She listened to the answer and announced, "Well, he's not working for you anymore." Without a waiting for a response, she hung up the phone with a crash.

I needed to find a new job. Soon, I hoped.

Our one bedroom apartment eventually felt cramped and awkward for four people. Esther knew I was a hard-working man that would soon provide better. I had seen so many people struggle with the most difficult, challenging experiences imaginable, and yet not just survive but find the strength, drive, and fortitude to forge ahead. Having been through that myself, I had little doubt I could overcome this challenge as well.

What's more, for any man who lost all his family in the war, the new family he creates is a kind of rebirth. My wife and my daughters were more than precious to me. They were a kind of life-force that made the most ordinary day seem like cause for celebration. The four of us were close-knit. It felt like the universe had played a trick on me. All of my family was taken away from me, and when I had suffered enough, I was given another one.

We continued to have very different feelings about religion. I was still confused about my belief in God. And if God did exist, then I was angry with him, very, very angry. No loving God could have allowed His people to endure what I had endured during the war, what all the people around me had endured. I did not have any answers. I did not have any substitute to believe in place of the certainty there was a God. That part of life was empty for me. Whether or not God existed, I did not want to have anything to do with religion.

I was blessed to have Esther. I called her Estherel. The last added syllable meaning "small" in Yiddish. She was considerate, good-hearted, lovable, and always looking for ways to be helpful to everyone around her.

Still, she was always uncomfortable at the High Holidays. I would not go to services with the family. Esther and the girls went, but they went without me. Esther tried to explain my absence to the children by telling them a story she made up. "Your father doesn't go to services because it reminds him of the family he lost in the war. It's too painful for him." She couldn't bring herself to tell them the truth, that I was angry with God.

At the end of the war, I could not handle the painful, gnawing truth that the rest of my family was gone, and I remained. This pain afflicted many of the other young survivors.

Back then, I often felt the need to share my anger with God with my friends. Sometimes I felt as if I was doing myself a favor by opening up about this terribly painful subject. But the easing of the pain only lasted as long as it took for the words to come out of my mouth. Nothing anyone said provided the slightest bit of healing or reassurance.

For a long time, I thought the only way I could avoid the pain was not to think about it. Have you ever tried to push something important or haunting out of your mind? It is a vicious circle. It is laughable. When you tell yourself, "I won't think about this," you are already thinking about it. I would try to force my brain to think about something else. But that is a senseless, self-defeating exercise. I was suffering, and there seemed to be no peace from the pain.

We signed up ten-year-old Frida for the neighborhood public school. She was miserable. Born in Israel, Hebrew was her first language, then French and then Spanish. Now, she was in America sitting in class barely able to understand anything the teacher said. Her sad face tore at me when I came home each evening. Each day I hoped the next would be better, that the sadness would wash away. Yet each day she came home just as defeated as the day before and the day before that. How long would it take?

Luckily, she quickly made friends with a classmate, a girl whose first language was Spanish. Because they shared that language, they became close friends, and she helped Frida through the hurdles of learning English. Within only a few months, our Frida excelled in her studies.

For newcomers, it can be valuable to live in a neighborhood of people with similar background—Mexican, Asian, Black, or Jewish. After Esther had arranged for me to be jobless, I spread the word around the Jewish neighborhood where we lived that I was a house painter. I found a few jobs, and soon after, satisfied customers told other people about me. Enough jobs came in to pay the bills.

The four of us had been in America for about nine months when we received the terrible news that President John F. Kennedy had been shot and killed. Esther and I were deeply saddened by the news. I thought the girls were too young to be affected, but both of them cried through most of the night, making my pain and Esther's all the greater. How do you tell young children that it's okay and everything will be all right when you don't believe it yourself?

I thought all the death I had witnessed would have hardened me to the death of a single person. I was greatly relieved to find it had not.

Looking back, Esther and I, as well as the children, adjusted to life in America like a snap of the fingers. In France and Mexico, we had been like tourists, but the United States felt like "the last station." We came to know people who seemed like they would be lifelong friends and who seemed like people we had known all our lives. We didn't wonder, "What next?" We found the country where we would spend the rest of our lives. America brought a sense of security, a sense I had not felt so deeply since leaving Israel.

House painting provided enough income that we didn't have to reach into our savings. One of the great gifts in life is to spend your days doing work that gives you satisfaction and a sense of achievement. House painting didn't bring me either of those. At the end of each job, I would wash my hands and tell myself, "This is the last one." Still, I was making good money, decent money.

Then one day after I had been house painting for about six months, I painted the house of a Czech woman, Mrs. Kaufman. She was a heavy-set lady who looked to me like a farmer's wife but seemed to outclass her dull husband. They were Holocaust survivors, which made me feel close to her, and to a lesser degree, her slow-witted husband. They were both good people, who made their living by renting out space in several apartment buildings they owned. Sometimes she watched me while I worked, and we chatted. At one point, she said, "Miki, you are not a painter."

I replied, "You are insulting me."

"No, no, no," she said. "You are very clean. You are an excellent painter. But you are something else. You are more educated."

I said, "I'm not educated at all. Remember, I'm a concentration camp survivor."

"But you are different," she explained. "Go back to looking for a job as an oil driller, but this time, don't say you're a Jew. Don't say you learned drilling in Israel."

Her words stunned me. This was America. Could being Jewish really make a difference in this great country? In France, we never experienced anti-Semitism. In Mexico, the locals talked about the "judíos" (Jews). They would say things like, he drives a big car, or he has a lot of money, so he must be a judío. But I never felt it was an insult; it simply felt like envy.

I took Mrs. Kaufman's advice and went to visit other oil companies with offices in Los Angeles. One was Western Geophysical, a firm that explored new sites for oil companies.

As a test, they sent me out to manage a night shift of six people at Signal Hill, right in Los Angeles.

It was all familiar to me, and the man sent to observe saw that I knew what I was doing. The next day, the company called to say I was hired and describe the drilling site where I would work. The pay was something like $270 a week, a very good salary in those days.

Yet I was disappointed and embarrassed. To get this job, I had to hide my Jewishness. Whether or not I believed in God, I was and still am a very proud Jew. It was against my nature and beliefs to hide this fundamental truth about who I am. I was happy to have the job, yes, certainly. But I was not proud of what I did to get it.

I put the emotional pain behind me and left the next day for the seven hour drive to a drilling site located north of Sacramento.

I was back to being a driller again, in charge of a crew of hardworking roughnecks. To look for oil, we drilled down about three hundred meters, pulled out the drill, planted dynamite at the bottom of the drill hole, and set it off. We then recovered soil samples, which were sent to the company's lab for evaluation.

People find it surprising when I tell them that roughnecks love the work. It wasn't like sitting at a desk eight hours a day or putting cans on the shelf at a supermarket. It required muscle, and it involved some danger if someone got careless or wasn't paying close attention. But it was men's work, and they found it satisfying.

I was very glad to have the job, yet it meant being away from the family for the entire work week. We wrapped up about five o'clock on Friday, so I didn't get to bed at home until after midnight. Then, I left again every Sunday afternoon for the long drive back. I hated being away from my wife and children five days every week.

My English was still limited, and I was only thirty-two years old, running a crew in their forties and fifties. But I learn very fast, a trait inherited from my father and one especially strong in many survivors.

When I got home for the weekend, Esther always had activities planned. All four of us liked to be active. We typically went swimming, boating, or fishing together at the Santa Monica beach. Sometimes we went to a place like Malibu hills and camped out overnight. Esther quickly became friendly with a lot of Israeli families, so weekends often included socializing as well.

Our happy life went into turmoil in 1964 when Esther gave birth to our third child, another daughter, Vivian. She was born three months premature and was so tiny that the doctors said she would not live. In fact, we learned later that she was the frailest infant ever to survive at the time. With a birth weight of under two pounds, she actually lost weight on her first day of life, but then she began to recover. She spent her first three months at the hospital in an incubator. Esther somehow managed to be very strong through this, while I secretly suffered in despair.

We brought her home, and she appeared to be happy and develop normally. At six months, she started to crawl in an awkward, clumsy way with her legs curled up. As soon as we noticed this, Esther made an appointment with the doctor. She called me that night at my motel near the oil fields, sobbing, and told me, "The doctor says she will probably never be able to walk."

After all I had been through and still struggling to shake off the devastating memories of the concentration camps, the news about our beautiful but deformed child shattered my life completely. I suffered something like a nervous breakdown.

While I was still dealing with this shattering news, I walked into the motel room I shared with my assistant one evening. He was a good worker and what you would call a hillbilly, likable enough but a lightweight in the intelligence department. He was watching the television show, *Combat*, about American troops in Germany during World War II. I sat down to watch and loved it—Americans killing the Germans. After a few minutes, my roommate said, "You know, I'm German."

I was shocked. He could only have meant his parents or grandparents were from Germany, but the way he said it stunned me. "I'm German," as if he had been born and brought up there, with a tinge of pride as if he wished the Germans had won the war. I did not show any reaction, but I was exploding inside. I was not a calm person in those days. I was hotheaded and had been that way since the first train ride to the concentration camp. Perhaps, it's an important part of what has kept me alive.

I did not let the German anti-Semite sense my fury but simply rolled up my sleeve and showed him my tattoo. I said, "I'm Jewish.

Look what the Germans did to me."

Incredibly, he did not know what the tattoo represented. I had to explain it. He showed no reaction. All he cared about apparently was that he now knew I was a Jew.

When I walked into breakfast the next morning, everything had changed. My entire crew looked at me with unbelievable hostility as if the devil himself walked through the door. I was still their boss, but obviously, I had become "the Jew."

From that day forward, they sabotaged my work. Out at the rigs, they made my life miserable in every way they could. When I needed the pipes pulled out, I yelled, and no one responded. They stole gas from my truck, so I suddenly found myself stranded out in the oil fields. Their anti-Semitism overwhelmed me.

The day came when one of the roughnecks on a truck refused to carry out the routine task I told him to do. Furious, I grabbed a twenty-four inch wrench and shouted, "Turn this truck around, or this wrench will be in your head." He did, oozing with hostility.

It was enough. I called the company and told my boss I quit. He tried to calm me down and begged me not to leave. I understood. I was qualified. I was valuable. I was making them money. But I suffered enough hatred in my life. I would not stay.

In so many ways, I found America like a dream, a place where anyone with drive and determination could build a fulfilling life. It was a cruel disappointment to find such deep rooted anti-Semitism.

By quitting the drilling job, I was out of work in the occupation I was best qualified for and where I earned significantly more than any other job I had been able to get. My personal life was still difficult as well. I was not yet able to put behind me the horrors of the war years. Worse, for reasons I still do not understand, I found living in the United States much more difficult than my early years in Slovakia or the years I spent in Israel, France, and even Mexico. I often fumed with anger, and I was tormented and unable to listen to anyone who wanted to help me. I only found peace when I worked or was with Esther and my children. Otherwise, it was like I was constantly boiling. It was difficult to stay calm and control myself.

The nights were even worse, still filled with terrifying nightmares. Once, after a senseless argument with a man, I saw him in my dreams that night as a German soldier, an SS man.

LIVES OF LOVE

What could I do for income? I knew I wasn't a skilled housepainter, but I was worried and desperate. It seemed like the only good choice. So once again I became a housepainter, but I decided I had learned enough about the business to go into it on my own. I bought the ladders, brushes, and other equipment I needed, including an old housepainter's truck.

On the side of the truck, I advertised that I did "painting, dekorating, and wallpapring." Below the misspelled items, it said: We may be spelling it wrong but we're doing it right. When I parked my truck in the neighborhood, people saw that, and it made them laugh.

One older Jewish lady told me, "I like it, I like it, I like it!"

She started to write down the phone number, and I said, "You don't have to write down the number—it's me!" I painted for her, and she recommended me to others. In no time, I had plenty of work. Soon I had to hire a couple of helpers.

For the next five years, I was a successful housepainter with enough work to keep myself and my hired crews busy, while providing a decent income for me and my family.

Our Vivian, who the doctors had said would not survive, grew up to be a strong, healthy, and happy child. Thankfully, her diagnosis proved to be inaccurate. She has only experienced a slight limp that has affected her life very little.

Through the years, I continued to have the horrible, depressing nightmares. Finally, Esther decided to take action. She scouted around and learned about a program for Holocaust survivors at UCLA.

She told me about it and encouraged me to go. I refused. I had been through so much. How could a pack of doctors who had not witnessed the unspeakable terrors possibly wipe away those terrible, painful memories? They had learning, but they did not have magic.

Without telling me, she went to talk to the doctors. That evening after dinner, she shared their advice. They recommended I go back and visit the concentration camps. They said this helped many survivors who experienced nightmares.

I can be stubborn. It took a lot of convincing until I finally agreed and booked a charter flight for us.

On board the plane, after everyone was seated and strapped in, I noticed an insignia mounted on one wall displaying some text and a small German flag. I called the stewardess and told her to get our bags off, we were not going to fly on a German plane. After some back and forth, she went to talk to the pilot, who came to speak with me. I told him I was a survivor and was not going to fly on a German plane. The other passengers were fidgeting and annoyed that we weren't even taxiing yet, but he brought me forward to see the flag close up along with the plaque that showed this charter aircraft wasn't owned by a German company. It was owned by Bank of America. Convinced, I thanked him. He surprised me with a friendly hug before escorting me back to my seat.

The trip did not start off well. Once we settled into our first hotel, my passions erupted. I hated the Germans so much that I found myself shouting at waiters, cab drivers, and hotel desk clerks.

All of that changed when we visited the camps. This proved to be a shattering experience yet life-changing. At Crematorium #2 in Auschwitz, where my mother and younger brother died, I lost control. The tears flowed and flowed. I could not stop crying. That evening I realized I had crossed a threshold. Something I thought was impossible occurred—I felt a sense of relief at last.

After Auschwitz, we went to Dachau. This was the most painful part of the trip. We visited the nearby site of the mass grave where my father and Andrew were buried. In my life, I had known such intense heartbreak, and this was the most painful of all—to know how needlessly they died at the very end of the war.

Miki and Esther at Auschwitz

I am blessed to have a grave for my father and my brother. For other survivors, there are thousands and thousands of graves in Poland and Germany that are marked with nothing more than a number. No one knows who lies beneath those markers. Even though my family graves are in Germany, I know where their bodies lie.

Miki and Esther at Mühldorf

After we left the camps, we flew to Israel. I wrote to a couple of my old friends from my Israeli military and Israeli oil drilling days that we planned to detour to Israel before returning home. When we arrived, more than a dozen friends that Esther and I knew in those early days of Israel were at the Tel Aviv airport to greet us, showering us with handshakes, hugs, and smiles.

We spent the next ten days visiting with these friends and visiting the special attractions of this land where Esther and I met and married. Israel seemed like a different country to us, more modern and much more prosperous. Our old friends were well off financially, and the nation was clearly thriving.

While I had no regrets of leaving, this was an emotional experience for me and for Esther as well. The days we spent trading memories and catching up with these companions of long ago helped to alleviate the dark memories that our visit to the camps revived.

When we got home from the trip, I found the nightmares ended. I stopped waking up at night crying. I stopped arguing and yelling at Esther. The advice of those experts at UCLA had proven to be miraculously valid.

We have since visited the camps four more times. The experience was very different. On these later trips, I wanted to go so intensely I could hardly wait for the plane to land. It no longer felt depressing or upsetting to me. On the contrary, it was a chance to measure how far I had come emotionally. My life vastly improved with those visits, and yet another surprising life change was on the horizon.

After a freak car accident that took me four months to recover from, it was clear that I was not able to go back to a job that involved physical labor and climbing ladders. But sometimes the answers to our biggest problems fall out of the sky. A friend told me I should take a look at the car wash business. He said, "You're a good mechanic. This would be a good business for you."

I already knew that another friend of mine, Scotty, was looking for a business. He liked the idea, and we agreed to find a car wash to buy together. In particular, a car wash that wasn't in good condition and could be bought for an affordable price. We would buy it, fix it up, and run it as partners. To me that made a lot of sense.

We found a place for sale with an asking price of only $85,000, a reasonable price given its rundown condition. Esther objected strongly, arguing that my share of the $30,000 down payment would take all of the savings we had left. Worse, it would leave us without enough money to pay the property tax bill on our home that was coming due.

Her forecast of doom and disaster proved wrong. My partner and I made a good choice. As we had planned, we were able to keep the car wash working and the cash flowing while I rebuilt and made the needed improvements. Though I knew nothing about car wash equipment, all those mechanical skills I gathered as an oil driller were put to work once again.

The only problem was in my choice of a partner. He turned out to be a "silent investor" who didn't want to get his hands dirty, leaving all the physical labor to me.

The partnership arrangement didn't get any better. I put the business up for sale and had no problem finding a buyer. The sale price was more than I could have dreamed. Fixing the place had demanded a lot of intense planning, supervising, and physical labor by me, but the business sold for a price that provided an astounding profit of some $40,000.

After the successful sale of the first car wash, I learned enough about the business that I turned around and bought another one on my own. Again, I fixed it up and resold it for a handsome profit. What started as something of a gamble turned into the beginning of a new career. Over the next thirty-seven years, I made an excellent living buying, fixing up, and selling car washes.

At age seventy-five, I decided to sell my last car wash and retire. By then our daughters had finished their education. Frida, the eldest, graduated from UCLA and spent a term at Cambridge on a scholarship. Vivian and Anita both have degrees from the University of California, Northridge. Through the years, I teased them that my university was Auschwitz. Perhaps you can appreciate how much it means to a man who had no formal education beyond age thirteen to be able to provide a good education for all three of my children.

Showing off our first grandson, 1982

I have always been so active that when I shared my plans to retire, my children feared how I would fill my days with no business to run. Frida, an attorney, had connections at the Los Angeles Holocaust Museum, called the Museum of Tolerance. She sent in an application that proposed I serve as a guest lecturer. They only wanted to know, "When can he start?"

The first few times I spoke at the museum recounting the things I most wanted to forget were harrowing and painful. As I continued with my speeches, the emotional drain lessened. Yet even today, after all these years, my talks still take an emotional toll. But as difficult as it is to talk about those ghastly times, I think it is even more difficult for people to hear about them. Even so, people crowd in for every lecture, sometimes in large numbers. I hope these visitors leave with the message that despite the hardships that are inevitable at times in our lives, we can still grow to live lives of love.

As I reviewed the final pages of this book, I received word that Robert Wasserberger had died. He was the last Holocaust survivor I knew from the concentration camps, the boy I had risked my life for by telling him to grab my pants when he was about to fall from weakness and fatigue.

It is deeply saddening to live with the knowledge that so few survivors are still alive and able to recount the stories of those horrible times. If we forget the past, today's generation and future generations are all the more likely to repeat some aspects of the terrors that mankind is capable of inflicting. And of course, on a smaller scale, these tragedies are still being repeated every day in various parts of the world.

I hope the painful story I have recounted here may help remind people today and in the future to be on their guard against savagery of every sort.

Michael ("Miki") Popik

EPILOGUE
My Daughters Remember

When my father first told me stories of the war years, I know that he watered them down to avoid anything gruesome or scary. Even when I was older, he never told me about the horrors. The stories he shared were like an adventure. In later years, remembering those conversations, I would tell people, "He made it sound funny."

It wasn't until my junior high years that I learned the truth of what life was like in the Nazi camps. I became friends with a girl a few years older whose father was also a survivor. She told me, "We're not like other people," and gave me a book to read about the war years. It was the first time I began to understand why my father was different and how he had been protecting me and my sisters.

Despite what he had been through, or maybe because of it, he was more passionate than other parents. And he was funnier. I remember my parents having ridiculous, stupid fights like children, fighting over nonsense.

But I also remember my father and mother as having what I sometimes describe as "an insanely passionate relationship"—what most people hope for but never get.

~ Frida

Because my father was so young when in the concentration camps, he was different from the other survivors I have met, in the way he grasped life and in the way he was determined to live a full life, putting fear behind him. That's how I always saw him, so the first time I heard him lecture at the Museum of Tolerance was a traumatic experience.

Knowing he was a Holocaust survivor wasn't much preparation for what I heard that day. He had made a point of never sharing the most gruesome stories with us. I cried hearing him tell stories of what he had gone through, but I also smiled. I smiled because he was still alive.

Our dad wanted his children never to feel that life is a struggle, so he believed in doing everything larger than life. We traveled, he was generous in giving us presents, he insisted on having way too much food on the table at every meal, and he never talked about the Holocaust.

When I was old enough to hear the real stories he had been hiding, I found it very painful, yet I was proud to have a father who had not only survived but who seemed to live life to the very fullest.

After he opened up, our mother did as well, and we learned how much she had endured in helping him survive the memories of those years. She was a crutch but he had never let us feel that. She kept him happy and strong, never letting us know about his terrible nightmares.

Even through the years when I now know he was struggling, he never let us see it. Growing up with no remaining family made him a man who strived all the harder for his wife and children. Even when he was suffering with jobs he got no satisfaction from, he didn't let us see it. Through the years I've met other children of survivors and found them to be people who were suspicious, living with fears. Our dad taught us to live to the fullest.

My sisters and I could never explain the feelings of being a survivor's daughter. But most people don't really want to know. Only one person ever asked, a school friend writing a paper. I grabbed her hand and thanked her, saying, "That was the most telling request you could have made."

Many times after his lecture at the Museum and elsewhere, I have seen grown men hugging him, just as I now know co-author Bill Simon did when he first heard my father speak. I feel proud of being the daughter of a man who has become a hero to so many people.

The most important thing I learned from my father:
Live life to the fullest, love life, and make a difference.

~ Anita

I knew that dad had terrible nightmares but he would not talk about them or offer any explanation, at least not when I was around. I knew he was a "survivor," but I didn't really know what the term meant, and he would not talk about it. Once he got a letter from a friend in Europe that had a picture of some schoolgirls. He looked at the picture and broke out in tears, one of the girls was his mother. I think he didn't like it that he had cried in front of me. It was many years before I ever saw him cry again.

On vacations we would often drive to California places like Big Bear or Lake Tahoe. I would climb into the front seat to listen to his stories of the hard times after his town had been taken over—stories of his high jinx, adventures, and the amusing parts of his struggles to survive. He never made it not sound dangerous or threatening. Just kids getting into mischief.

Besides dad's nightmares, as he got older, he began to be fussy about food. For example, he insisted on having fresh-baked bread for dinner every evening … even if the main course was pasta or another carbohydrate. He'd often eat half a loaf of bread at a single meal. I finally decided that given his experience in the camps, bread was life. Today, we still have to make trips to the bakery for fresh bread at dinner.

About 1975, we moved to a new house, the house that my parents still live in. The old place and the new one were just a few miles apart but a world apart in character: We had left behind the immigrant setting for middle-class America. For me and my sisters, it was an introduction to a world we didn't know existed. In the homes of our new friends, the parents said hello but didn't talk to us.

We hadn't been there long before I realized that where the neighborhood kids wanted to hang out was at our house. The whole atmosphere was different. Mother was a singer, and sang for us. She provided food, because "Food is love." When dad came home, he would keep us all entranced with his stories and jokes. Was it a conscious attempt to create feelings so removed from what he had known in the camps? I still don't know, but he made it fun.

After his first visit to Auschwitz, our father started filling us in on the more painful stories of his childhood. That solved an issue for me and my sisters. It had been weird. Kids want to know about their parents' childhood, and up until then our dad had never been willing to share the aching, haunting parts of his story.

I think our father, and our mom as well, have done remarkably better than most survivors and their partners—maybe because they embraced the promises of the American dream, the idea that with hard work and dedication, you can achieve a life worth living.

What I most admire about my father is that he has built for himself and his family a life of everything that during the war they tried to take away from him. And I have moved through life guided by his principle that you can achieve almost anything you want if you are dedicated enough.

~ Vivian

Esther and the girls, 1990

Miki and Esther on their way to a party, 2000

Miki and Esther with their family

ACKNOWLEDGMENTS

The life I live now, and the peace of mind I have achieved, have been made possible by my patient, understanding, supportive, and gentle wife, Esther. I am grateful to her for putting up with me, standing by me, and guiding me through some very difficult times. And I am grateful to my three educated, successful daughters who have turned out so well despite—or perhaps because of—the life lessons their father learned under the worst of circumstances. The four of them have helped to make me whole and treasure life again.

Finally, I owe a great debt to my co-author, New York Times bestselling author William L. Simon. Bill heard one of my lectures at the Museum of Tolerance in Los Angeles. After the lecture, he approached me and made a request that many others have made of me before and since, "May I hug you?" He felt so moved that he told me if I wasn't already writing a book about my experiences, he wanted to write the story with me. He did this without compensation and explained, "It was something I felt compelled to do. Miki's story is just too powerful not to be part of the permanent record of the Holocaust."

Printed in Great Britain
by Amazon

16163787R00058